National Children's Bureau seri...

Editor: Mia Kellmer Pringle

This new series examines contemporary issues relating to the development of children and their needs in the family, school and society. Based on recent research and taking account of current practice, it also discusses policy implications for the education, health and social services. The series is relevant not only for professional workers, administrators, researchers and students but also for parents and those involved in self-help movements and consumer groups.

Published

Caring for Separated Children
R. A. Parker (editor)

A Fairer Future for Children
Mia Kellmer Pringle

Children in Changing Families: a Study of Adoption and Illegitimacy
Lydia Lambert and Jane Streather

Forthcoming

Combined Nursery Centres: a New Approach to Education and Day Care
Elsa Ferri, Dorothy Birchall, Virginia Gingell and Caroline Gipps

Children in Changing Families

A Study of Adoption and Illegitimacy

Lydia Lambert
and
Jane Streather

© National Children's Bureau 1980

All rights reserved. No part of this publication may be repro-
duced or transmitted, in any form or by any means, without
permission.

First published 1980 by
THE MACMILLAN PRESS LTD
London and Basingstoke
Associated companies in Delhi Dublin
Hong Kong Johannesburg Lagos Melbourne
New York Singapore and Tokyo

Printed in Hong Kong

British Library Cataloguing in Publication Data

Lambert, Lydia
    Children in changing families.
    1. Child development – Great Britain
    2. Adoption – Great Britain
    3. Illegitimacy – Great Britain
    I. Title   II. Streather, Jane
    III. National Children's Bureau
    155.4   HQ792.G7

    ISBN 0–333–28696–0
    ISBN 0–333–28697–9 Pbk

This book is sold subject to the standard conditions of the Net
Book Agreement.

The paperback edition of this book is sold subject to the
condition that it shall not, by way of trade or otherwise, be lent,
resold, hired out, or otherwise circulated without the publisher's
prior consent in any form of binding or cover other than that in
which it is published and without a similar condition including
this condition being imposed on the subsequent purchaser.

Contents

Part II   The Children at 11: their Families and Environments

Part III The Children at 11: their Development and Progress since 7

Part IV Fitting the Patterns Together

List of Tables and Figures

Tables in Appendix 2

Please note that tables are referenced as follows:

Table 6.1   = Table in text
Table A6.1 = Appendix table (see Appendix 2)
Table S6.1 = Supplementary table (see Appendix 3)

Acknowledgements

Firstly, we would like to thank our sponsors, The Buttle Trust, Noel Buxton Trust, Children's Research Fund, City Parochial Foundation, and an anonymous trust, for their generous support.
    Secondly, we would like to thank all our colleagues at the National Children's Bureau who have had a hand in producing this report. Every Bureau publication is, to a greater or lesser extent, a joint venture, but there are some people we would like to mention and thank specifically. Peter Wedge has been involved throughout and given patiently and generously of his time, as has Ken Fogelman in the later stages. Harvey Goldstein was statistician to the project till he left the Bureau, when his place was taken over by Jenny Head. Ian Vallender and Biddy Cunnell have helped with the references and among the typists Roz Treadway, Celia Rodbard, Joyce Famosa, Bobbie Reddaway, Esther Mason, Judy Angus and especially Diane Haggis gave particular assistance. Mia Pringle, Joan Cooper, Elsa Ferri, Dougal Hutchison, Juliet Essen, Doria Pilling and also Jane Rowe (from ABAFA) read the main draft in record time and made many valuable comments.
    Finally, we should explain that the authorship is joint in spirit rather than in time. Lydia came to the project when it received a six months' extension and took over from Jane a great pile of material, which forms the basis of this book. Jane had spent 16 months working on the project and continued to give some of her busy time till the end but Lydia is responsible for the book's final shape and contents. We are united in a common concern for our subjects and would like to offer our thanks and good wishes to all those who are in the National Child Development Study.

Part I

Changing Patterns in Society and the Family

1

Introduction

Illegitimacy and adoption are two subjects which have constantly aroused people's interest, however furtively, during the twentieth century. Both have a history going back into the mists of time but in Britain adoption became formally recognised with the passing of the first Adoption Acts in 1926 (England) and 1930 (Scotland). These made provision for *de facto* situations which had increased considerably with the number of children left fatherless (not all of them were illegitimate) by the 1914–18 war.

Once on the statute book, adoption came to be seen by some as a means of covering up illegitimacy, and by others as the solution to childlessness (McWhinnie, 1967). Adoption was also seen as a way of legalising the position of children joining families which had been reconstituted by new marriages. Thus, from the start, adoption was considered a respectable way of resolving situations intimately bound up with men and women's sexuality and their roles in society, and with the constitution and functions of the family. Knowing that it was a man-made creation, people have been very concerned to find out how adoption has turned out, both for the children and for the families adopting them. At the same time there has been a continuing interest in, and concern for, illegitimate children who are not adopted (Gill, 1977). This interest, too, is bound up with sexuality and morality, with family and societal structures and also with the practical considerations arising from such births.

On many occasions adopted and illegitimate children have been studied, as separate groups or in comparison with each other, but there is also a need to compare both groups with legitimately born children for a fuller understanding of the dynamics of child development. One such opportunity has presented itself through the study carried out by the National Children's Bureau of all the children living in England, Scotland and Wales who were born in the first week of March 1958 (the National Child Development Study). In two parallel reports the families, backgrounds and development of the illegitimately born and of the adopted children have already been described up to the age of 7 (Crellin *et al.*, 1971; Seglow *et al.*, 1972). The circumstances surrounding the placements for adoption, and the adopters' views of how the children had progressed since then, were the subjects of a special interview enquiry which provided additional data for the report on the adopted children (Seglow *et al.*, 1972).

At the time when the illegitimate children were born, the mothers came from similar social class backgrounds as those who were married, but they tended to be younger than average and their babies were more likely to be lower in birthweight (Crellin *et al.*, 1971). By the age of 7 the majority of the children who had been adopted were living in surroundings which, relatively speaking, were socially and materially advantageous, while illegitimate children who had not been adopted tended to live in circumstances which were disadvantageous.

The school attainment at 7 of adopted children was generally as good as, or slightly better than, that of legitimately born children, and significantly better than that of children who had been born illegitimately but who had not been adopted. As far as social adjustment at school and at home was concerned the adopted children gave some indications of behaviour difficulties when compared with legitimate children, but not as many as the illegitimate children, who showed significantly disturbed behaviour at school and at home (Crellin *et al.*, 1971; Seglow *et al.*, 1972).

In general terms the findings up to the age of 7 were considered to have demonstrated that adoption was a very satisfactory means of providing care for children whose mothers were not able to keep them. The illegitimately born children who were not placed for adoption were, as a group, growing up in more difficult social circumstances and their relatively poorer attainment and social adjustment suggested the need for much enhanced support services for these children and their families.

Because one report highlighted the positive features of adoption and the other stressed the adverse circumstances of illegitimate children, they were interpreted by some readers as polarising the situations in a way which implied a value judgement that adoption was 'better' than keeping one's illegitimate child. In fact, both reports offered some reassurance to the natural parents who had had to make the decision whether to part with their children. On the one hand those mothers who had given up their babies for adoption could know that their children were developing well while, on the other hand, those who decided to keep their children could see that the environmental pressures with which they had to cope were recognised. In any case the seven-year findings were not intended as a final statement. Although the importance of the early years of childhood has been constantly demonstrated, the years leading to puberty, adolescence and to adulthood have their own special places in child development, and it was always the researchers' hope that further studies of these two groups would be possible (Seglow *et al.*, 1972).

The purpose of the present report is, therefore, to look at the illegitimate and adopted children at the age of 11 and to consider changes in their background and development since the age of 7 in comparison with children who were legitimately born. In doing so, the intention is to look more closely at the changing patterns of family life for both illegitimate and legitimate children and to set these changes within an environmental context. Only by doing this can some understanding be gained of the continuing importance, or unimportance, of birth status and of the processes at work in our society.

The chapters which follow provide reference points and background to the detailed findings on these children. They set the scene and discuss some of the issues which arise more specifically later on. First, we shall consider environmental factors which are associated with child development; second, we shall explore the role and function of the family in contemporary society, before considering illegitimacy and adoption as such; third, we outline our approach to the study and present findings from it; and, finally, we bring all the strands together and draw some conclusions.

2

The Environment and Child Development

The powerful influence of the environment in facilitating or hindering child development is a necessary concern in this study of changing families. Much research in recent years has shown the importance of social factors in contributing to health, educational attainment, job opportunities and life chances of all kinds (for example, Spence, *et al.*, 1954; Miller, *et al.*, 1974; Douglas, 1964; Douglas *et al.*, 1968; Davie *et al.*, 1972; Wedge and Prosser, 1973).

The concept of environment is an ambiguous one, and has been approached in a number of different ways, often depending on the disciplinary orientation of the researchers. Nevertheless, a number of key elements can be identified, including social class; home circumstances (for example, family structure and size, the social and educational background of the parents, the parents' relationship with each other and their children, their methods of child-rearing, and parental aspirations for their children); command over basic resources such as income and housing; and the more nebulous but discernible effects of privilege or stigma (for example, Schorr, 1964; Newson and Newson, 1974; Pringle, 1974; Holman 1970a; Wilson and Herbert, 1978).

The way in which these elements are combined helps to determine the influence of the environment on a particular child, although, as will be seen, this may not always be in the expected direction or be irreversible. The interaction of such factors is complex and their relationship to development not fully understood yet. This does not deny the relevance of heredity, but if any justification is required for concentrating on environmental factors, it is because they are more amenable to change. Irrefutably the opportunities, choices and life chances which contribute to children's development are not fixed at birth; and it is precisely the circumstances surrounding the birth of the children who were born illegitimate and the interaction of these circumstances with their subsequent histories which form the focus of the current investigation.

The family situation is clearly of major importance in the present study, and so this element will be reviewed in a separate chapter. Before going on to look at some of the other relevant elements in the environment, we need to consider a further concept as it underlies much of the thinking in this study – namely, the concept of deprivation or disadvantage. In addition to, and also leading out of, a consideration of deprivation one should not overlook the positive effects of a 'good' environment.

Deprivation or disadvantage

Deprivation is perhaps one of the most ill-defined elements in the environment and, as Rutter and Madge (1976) point out, there is confusion as to whether the term deprivation refers to lack or loss. Strictly speaking, deprivation means loss, but it is frequently applied to situations where a family or a child has always lacked the advantages, material or otherwise, that most people take for granted. For this and other reasons Rutter and Madge prefer to use the term 'disadvantage', and in general the same broad meaning is used in the present study.

On the whole families who are deprived or disadvantaged tend to face multiple difficulties. For example, families living on low incomes are also likely to have inferior housing, and both low incomes and poor housing are often accompanied by cultural handicaps which relate particularly to child-rearing and socialisation. However, it is also possible for certain aspects of deprivation and disadvantage to occur in outwardly affluent and successful middle-class families, as has been shown in studies of child neglect and abuse (e.g. Helfer and Kempe, 1968; Oliver *et al.*, 1974).

There is no clear line marking out those who are disadvantaged and those who are not, despite crude measures such as the 'official poverty line' as defined by Supplementary Benefits Scale rates. Townsend (1970) has argued that poverty, for example, is a relative and dynamic concept and the same is true of other measures. The 'deprived' may be those who tend to have the least or worst of any particular aspect of life, or they may experience one or more disadvantages in an acute form. Many of the disadvantages described in this study are those that are typical among working-class families.

Influence of a 'good' environment

Some of the ambiguity within the concept of deprivation or disadvantage becomes obvious when considering adopted children who have suffered the loss (and often the lack) of their own parents, and perhaps other difficulties in early childhood, but have moved into situations which are in most respects highly advantageous. Adoption will be considered more fully in Chapter 5, but several studies, not just of adopted children, have shown that, even after early trauma, placement in a good environment can lead to a general increase in scores of measured intelligence and improved social adjustment (Clarke and Clarke, 1976).

The reversal of the effects of early adverse circumstances has, however, been a subject of controversy. In particular the notion of a 'critical period' in the early years of a child's development has been challenged. A number of studies in the 1940s indicated that abnormalities in development were irreversible and Bowlby, in particular, was pessimistic about the recovery of children from serious early psychological damage, and especially from prolonged mother–child separation (Goldfarb, 1943; Spitz, 1946; Bowlby, 1951). Current opinion is increasingly sceptical of such views, but it is acknowledged that much more research is needed before a full understanding of the mechanisms can be reached (Caldwell, 1970; Pringle, 1971; Rutter, 1972; Clarke and Clarke, 1976; Rutter and Madge, 1976).

Longitudinal and population studies of child development have tended to show that children living in a 'good' environment, whether defined by social class, material conditions, family size, parental interest or other factors, are the most likely to 'do well' in terms of attainment, adjustment and physical development (Douglas *et al.*, 1968; Davie *et al.*, 1972). Such findings raise important questions regarding the differences and similarities in development between illegitimate, adopted and legitimate children, and the extent to which these are related to the children's birth status or to other factors in their environment.

Social class

One way in which children's home backgrounds have been much categorised in studies of child development is by employing the concept of social class, a familiar notion in Britain. While common usage is made of terms such as 'working class', 'middle class' and 'upper class' in everyday life to refer to a person's position in society, and sometimes with their status, their worth, the term also has a more specific connotation. It describes the occupational group, as defined by the Registrar General for census purposes, of the male head of household. Broadly, social class, defined in this way, classifies and differentiates populations according to social background, characteristics, behaviour and values.

A number of studies have shown a strong association between social class and child development, and these findings are well documented and well known. Social class has been shown to be linked with obstetric care and birth risks such as perinatal and infant mortality and low birthweight (Illsley, 1955; Butler and Bonham, 1963). Despite reductions in infant mortality and morbidity, children born to working-class parents still have markedly higher risks of not surviving than children born to middle-class parents (Chamberlain *et al.*, 1975). It has also been shown that there is a relationship between social class and children's height, and both are linked with parity, family size, birthweight, and smoking in pregnancy (Spence *et al.*, 1954; Davie *et al.*, 1972).

Social class correlations with educational attainment have been much investigated (e.g. Floud *et al.*, 1956; Douglas *et al.*, 1968). It has been suggested that the social class differences stem from the variable amount of stimulation at home and also from some built-in advantages for middle-class children in that they find in the school substantially the same values as they experience at home. This is not to suggest that schools deliberately discriminate against working-class children; indeed, many schools positively discriminate in favour of them. However,

. . . by the time the children start school they have acquired an orientation to the world embracing norms and attitudes which affect their response to school. Many working class children will find these norms and attitudes are in significant respects different from those adopted by the school; they will tend to be judged by standards which are alien to their previous experience (Davie *et al.*, 1972).

Over a whole range of abilities test scores reflect a substantial division between the children from non-manual (or middle-class) homes on the one hand and those from manual (or working-class) homes on the other (Douglas *et al.*, 1968; Davie *et al.*, 1972; Fogelman *et al.*, 1978). Similarly it has been suggested that there are clear social class differences in speech and language, such as Bernstein's distinction between the 'elaborated' and the 'restricted' codes (for example, Bernstein, 1961, 1966). However, this contrast is by no means universally accepted (see Labov, 1969).

Although numerous studies have explored the ways in which styles of life are transmitted through the family and have focused on factors such as parental education, the family structure (particularly that of 'anomalous' families), working mothers, or parental attitudes, there is relatively little knowledge of the precise way in which class factors are mediated through the family and come to enhance or depress educational attainment. This is partly because not much attention has been given to the study of parental attitudes and behaviour in the context of environmental circumstances, particularly where these circumstances amount to deprivation. Although characteristics such as family size are assumed to be related to attitudes (for example, in the Plowden Report, CACE, 1967), it is rare to find attitudes being related to access to resources such as income and housing, and to experiences at work and in the community (Askham, 1975). Educational psychologists, teachers and others are aware of the importance of socialisation and especially of those aspects which relate to the inculcation of attitudes and behaviour in school, but they may not have given sufficient consideration to the relationship between parental attitudes and the difficulties faced by parents whose housing, for instance, is poor or whose income is low and insecure (Wilson, 1970).

Socialisation, relationships and child-rearing practices

Differences in child-rearing techniques have been linked with social class differences (e.g. Bronfenbrenner, 1958; Kohn, 1963; Newson and Newson, 1976). Middle-class parents are frequently described as 'permissive' and 'child-centred', and this has been related to their conditions of life and work, which allow them greater economic security and place more emphasis on interpersonal relations, self-direction and individual action. Working-class parents tend to be seen as more 'restrictive', and this has been related both to the need to strive for a respectable standard of living, and to the nature of their work, which depends on a collective approach, is standardised and supervised, and entails the 'manipulation of things' (Kohn, 1963).

Changes in child-rearing patterns have been noted among both middle-class and working-class families towards a 'child-centred' approach. To a large extent this may reflect the fact that middle-class and working-class parents share core values. The objectives of socialisation may be described as the production of healthy, affectionate, and responsible personalities able to cope with the demands of a mobile and industrial society (Parsons and Bales, 1956; Pringle, 1974). The degree of commitment to these values and the way they are carried out will vary, and not all families behave in ways which are consistent with them, but, broadly speaking, they represent the aims of the majority of families in this country. Poverty and stresses such as those engendered by an urban environment are factors which, however, tend to militate against them (Rodman, 1963; Wilson and Herbert, 1978).

Child-centred child-rearing practices have developed alongside a general rise in living standards. As families acquire a surplus over their basic needs, as their jobs, incomes and homes become more secure, parents are able to devote more attention to their children. Indeed, some would say that this trend has reached the point where children are 'taking over' their parents completely (Rapoport *et al.*, 1977). Nevertheless, there are groups in the population who, because of low wages, unemployment, sickness or other reasons, have not been able to experience the rise in material standards. The pressures of coping with these difficulties affect their whole attitude to life and make child-rearing problematic. Initiative, planning for the future and control over the immediate environment are all affected by adverse circumstances. Relationships between parents can become strained, and because of constraints on time and energy it also becomes more difficult, for example, to show affection to the children or to take an interest in their schooling and general progress (see Schorr, 1964; Jackson and Jones, 1971; Holman, 1970a).

Children with parents who are not able to spend much time with them may start school with a disadvantage, as they are likely to lack some of the basic social skills which would have enabled them to cope with the demands of school, and as the terms go by their disadvantage can easily become reinforced. This is particularly so if a child becomes labelled as being of 'poor ability' or as coming from a 'poor home'. If a child's identity and confidence are undermined, poor school progress can become a self-fulfilling prophecy and can, in turn, influence negative parental attitudes. Hence, by the time a child is 11 a combination of adverse circumstances and attitudes can build up into a disturbing vortex of disadvantage which is in stark contrast to the accumulation of advantages enjoyed by children living in more fortunate circumstances.

Income

Low income is perhaps one of the most obvious of the environmental disadvantages which interact with parental attitudes. During the 1960s, when wages and living standards in general were rising, there was a 'rediscovery' of family poverty (Abel-Smith and Townsend, 1965). In 1901 Rowntree had identified families with young children as being at risk from the effects of poverty and a similar situation still applied 60 years later. This fact was reflected in the birth of the Child Poverty Action Group in 1965, which, among other things, campaigned for the introduction of family allowances for first-born children (Bull, 1971).

While the full extent of poverty in Britain is not known exactly, among the particularly vulnerable are groups such as large families, fatherless families, families whose head is out of work or earning low wages (e.g. Wynn, 1964; MSS, 1967; SBC, 1967; Edmonds and Radice, 1968; Sinfield, 1968; Land, 1969; Hunt et al., 1973; Jordan, 1974; Wedderburn and Craig, 1974). These groups do not constitute a separate entity or class. If their circumstances are defined as poor relative to current standards of living, they are those 'individuals and families whose resources, over time, fall seriously short of the resources commanded by the average individual or family in the community in which they live' (Townsend, 1970). There are children in the study, described in this book, both legitimately and illegitimately born, living in one- and in two-parent families who can be identified as poor in this way.

Essentially there are two kinds of pressures that emanate from poverty – practical difficulties and stress – and these are usually interdependent. Difficulties in day-to-day living create stress, and stress makes it even more difficult for a family to cope with practical problems. For some it becomes almost impossible to achieve anything like the standards of domestic life and child-rearing that are expected by others who are living in more advantageous circumstances. As already noted, these stresses and strains are likely to be related to children's attainment and adjustment in school. They are also likely to be associated with physical development and health, for although poor families tend to spend a higher proportion of their income on food than more affluent families, the nutritional value of the diet is often lower and resistance to disease weaker (see Lambert, 1964; DEP, 1970; Bottomley, 1972; Marsden, 1973; Brown, 1974). The greater tendency for mothers in poor families to suffer from ill-health and depression is also likely to make child-rearing a more arduous task (Brown and Harris, 1978). For some the pressures become so great that they lead to family break-up and to the children being received into the care of the local authority (Holman, 1976). High-income families also have stresses and break down but they more rarely approach local authorities for help as they have other resources to draw on and other means of coping with difficulties (Packman, 1968; Pringle, 1974).

Lack of income, goods and services also means that poor families often find themselves unable to participate in activities which other people take for granted. This can lead to a sense of isolation and also to stigma and a low sense of self-worth (Pinker, 1971). In the past poor families usually had access to local support systems of kin and neighbours, but the break-up of communities into new environments has meant that both the practical help and the companionship these networks brought can be lacking (Willmott and Young, 1960). This makes it more difficult for poor families to socialise their children in all sorts of ways. While affluent families may also be cut off from the old networks, they are more likely to have the resources to travel back to them or to provide compensations.

Thus, much of what has been taken by some to be a separate culture is simply an adaptation to deprived conditions of life as epitomised by low income (Kriesberg, 1963; Valentine, 1968; Wilson, 1970; Ryan, 1971). If they had the same access to resources as higher-income families, few poor families would choose to maintain the way of life that poverty has forced them into and there would be immediate and also long-term benefits to their children (Kriesberg,

1970; Holman, 1973). This does not deny the fact that disadvantage can persist from one generation to another, though our knowledge of how this happens is limited (Galbraith, 1958; Orshansky, 1963; Rutter and Madge, 1976).

The poverty of certain groups is highlighted relative to the rising incomes and standards of living of the majority of families in Britain. Not all the results of this increase in wealth are beneficial, but there is no doubt that most families are able to provide better housing, better food and clothing and more leisure activities for their children than previous generations. Public expenditure on health care, education and facilities has also meant that, even for poor children, life chances are considerably improved. These very improvements constantly beg the questions of why it is necessary to maintain conditions of inequality and why some groups in particular should appear to be penalised. These questions are especially relevant for illegitimate children.

Housing

Poor housing is another of the environmental disadvantages which interact with parental attitudes. Many children in this country grow up in sub-standard and/or overcrowded accommodation (Essen and Fogelman, 1979). This fact and others relating to the extent of housing deprivation have emerged relatively recently, although there has been concern about housing standards for many years (Greve, 1964; Milner Holland Report, Ministry of Housing, 1965; Donnison, 1967; Woolf, 1967; Glastonbury, 1971; Francis Report, DOE, 1971). Housing quality may be measured in a number of ways, but among the most common are crowding and access to amenities, both of which have links with aspects of tenure.

Some of the worst overcrowding and poor physical amenity conditions are found in the privately rented housing sector, which also tends to be among the oldest part of the dwelling stock (Woolf, 1967; Field, 1974). There has been a decline in the private rented sector which has accelerated since the 1965 Rent Act. To some extent this is a welcome trend, but it has tended to increase the hardship for many families, particularly as both house prices and council rents have been rising during the same period. Despite legislation to improve security of tenure, there has always been a greater likelihood of homelessness among private tenants, particularly from furnished tenancies (Spencer, 1970). Ironically, this is also the type of accommodation which is often sought as an alternative to the official homelessness of local authority temporary accommodation. A relatively high proportion of one-parent families have lived in the private sector of housing (Holman, 1970b; Hunt *et al.*, 1973; Finer Report, DHSS, 1974; Ferri, 1976). For many of these families there has been no choice but to take the most overcrowded and dilapidated of furnished accommodation, often comprising one room and shared (if any) amenities (Blake, 1972; Catholic Housing Aid Society, 1972). One-parent families are particularly vulnerable to the risk of becoming homeless and some, unable to obtain any other accommodation at all, have to share with relatives or friends (Holman, 1975).

Council housing can vary enormously in quality, and although all the basic amenities are more likely to be provided than in the private sector, a considerable proportion of children living in council housing live in overcrowded homes (Essen and Parrinder, 1975). One reason for this is that a high proportion of large families are found in local authority housing because the points system for allocating council houses takes account of the numbers, ages and sex of the children. Although large families tend to get priority in rehousing, they are often placed in relatively poor accommodation, and in any event most of the dwellings available to the council only have two or three bedrooms, so that they are still likely to be overcrowded. Large families are also relatively more at risk of eviction and homelessness (but less now than in the past, owing to improved rent rebate schemes and legislation on homelessness) because these families are more likely to have financial problems and run into rent arrears. While the points system may improve the chances of rehousing for large families, it can discriminate against one-parent families. Even though the accommodation needs of the family with one parent are similar to those with two parents, the absence of one adult may reduce the number of points, and in some areas mothers and daughters, for example, have been expected to share a bedroom. One-parent families, like large families, have often been placed by local authorities in relatively poor accommodation and in neighbourhoods that have become run-down (see Land, 1969; Spencer, 1970).

In general, families living in owner-occupied homes are considered to be in the most fortunate position as they have security of tenure (unless they cannot keep up mortgage repayments) and are less likely to be overcrowded than families in the privately rented or the local authority sectors (Donnison, 1967). However, the quality of housing can vary as much as in the other sectors, and some owner-occupiers live in the oldest housing, which may well lack basic amenities or even be classified as 'unfit', or located in a slum or redevelopment area. One-parent families, particularly with lone mothers, are much less likely to be owner-occupiers than two-parent families (Finer, DHSS, 1974). There is also some evidence to suggest that even where they have been living in their own homes, one-parent families are likely to have to move out of them in cases of marital breakdown (Ferri, 1976; Tunnard, 1977). Sometimes the move may have preceded the break-up of the family, but in other cases mortgage foreclosure has been a precipitating factor.

Almost inevitably there is a relationship between poor housing and low income, as poverty places people in a weak bargaining position in the housing market. This is particularly true in the private sector, but even in the local authority sector families may be placed in, or moved to, older or sub-standard property if they are known to be unable to afford the higher rents of the better quality housing, or if there is a history of rent arrears (rent money is often used as the poor man's 'bank overdraft' in times of hardship). Rising expenditure on housing out of limited budgets has been linked with a deterioration in the diet of large families (Donnison, 1967).

Inadequate housing has also been associated with a poor perception of self, and with ill-health and tiredness in parents, which makes it difficult for them to give sufficient attention to their children (see Schorr, 1964). Privacy can become a real problem in overcrowded homes, and so can finding somewhere to put toys and playthings (if they can be afforded at all). Furthermore, if the neighbourhood is confined, there may be nowhere except the streets, derelict sites or the passages and stairs of high-rise blocks, where children can play outside the home. These limitations can retard children's development in a number of important ways and lead to a lack of stimulation and 'mental undernourishment', which may be as real a problem as physical undernourishment (Pringle, 1974). By contrast, children who live in good housing, with space (and money) for playthings and exercise, have a far greater opportunity to develop physically, mentally and socially (Davie *et al.*, 1972).

The evidence pertaining to factors in the environment, such as housing and income, clearly demonstrates that many children live their lives in or on the margins of poverty and in poor housing, particularly if they come from working-class backgrounds. The poverty that the children in such families experience goes beyond hardship and is known to be associated with their physical and social development and with their school attainment. Increasingly in our advanced industrial society education can be expected to be the key to occupational success, social status and good material standards of living. It is here that the children of manual workers, or those from large families or one-parent families, can 'lose out', because they tend to do less well at school and gain least from the educational system than children from more affluent and middle-class homes. Such findings are clearly important when exploring the development of illegitimate, of adopted and of legitimate children.

3

The Family

... there are some cogent reasons for believing that social life in general is never in a steady state of conflict – free equilibrium. There is always change, conflict, disagreement over means and ends and gaps between the ideal norm and the activities of everyday life. Rather than being the exception to the general state of social life, the family is best seen as a model of conflict, change and ambivalence . . . (Skolnick, *The Intimate Environment*, 1973, p. 435).

In our society the 'normal' or 'conventional' family has tended to be equated with the nuclear family, that is, with conjugal, small, independent households. Each individual family has been regarded as part of a system of interlocking nuclear families (Harris, 1969; Turner, 1969; Goode, 1964). Hence, in Britain, as in many other countries which have become industrialised, the family is thought to consist of two married parents and their dependent children, usually two, living in a household of their own (Laslett, 1972). The extent to which this is actually so in the mid-twentieth century, and, if it is not, how widespread the variations and the forms they take, has been questioned (for example, by Cogswell, 1975) and will be considered in the present study.

Talcott Parsons has been the major proponent of the conventional family. He and other social scientists constructed a model of the nuclear family with important societal functions as part of a balanced social system (see Parsons, 1949; Parsons and Bales, 1956). Rapoport *et al.* (1977) have commented that 'the conventional model assumed a Darwinian "fitness" of all of the elements to one another and to the environment'. Hence, the conventional family, according to the classical model, has the following elements (Rapoport *et al.*, 1977):

(i)   The male head of the household, the father, is the sole economic provider.
(ii) The female head of the household, the mother, is the home-maker, and responsible for domestic care and the socialisation of the children. She is a helpmeet to the husband, providing support for him in his struggle for the family's survival.
(iii) The children are helpless and dependent, vulnerable, and malleable. They must be nurtured full-time by the mother (or mother surrogate) only, as emotional stability is essential.
(iv) The family is a private institution and within it individuals can fulfil their most important needs. This fulfilment is based on the foundation of the economic income provided by the husband (where necessary, supplemented by the state). Only when economic and material needs have been met do expressions of psychological and social needs for love, esteem, self-expression and fulfilment emerge within the family.
(v)   Healthy families produce healthy individuals, who adjust to social roles.

The conventional model of the family embodies certain assumptions about how families should be. These have been summarised by Skolnick and Skolnick (1974):

(i)   the nuclear family – a man, a woman and their children – is universally found in every human society, past, present and future;
(ii) the nuclear family is the foundation of society, the key in-stitution guaranteeing the survival and stability of the whole society:
(iii) the nuclear family is the building block or elementary unit of society. Larger groupings – the extended family, the clan, the society – are combinations of nuclear families;
(iv) the nuclear family is based on a clear-cut, biologically structured division of labour between men and women, with the man playing the 'instrumental' role of breadwinner, provider and protector, and the woman playing the 'expressive' role of housekeeper and emotional mainstay;
(v)   a major 'function' of the family is to socialise children – that is,

to tame their impulses and instil values, skills and desires necessary to run the society. Without the nuclear family the adequate socialisation of human beings is impossible;

(vi) other family structures, such as mother and children, or the experimental commune, are regarded as deviant by the participants, as well as the rest of the society, and are fundamentally unstable and unworkable.

Some social scientists have identified a confusion of the empirical nuclear family with its idealised counterpart in the nuclear family ideology. Skolnick (1973), for example, regards the Parsonian model as 'utopian' because it sees the family as integrative and providing for continuity and stability as part of the utopian social system as a whole, and because it sees the family as a system of perfectly interlocking needs and a miniature utopian system in itself. Birdwhistell (1966) regards the conventional family model as 'sentimental'. While pointing out that he 'knows of no cases in which the ideal model has been observed', he notes that the key aspects of the sentimental model of the nuclear family include assumptions about the naturalness, emotional intensity, self-sufficiency and balance of the nuclear family unit.

The assumption that one form of family is not only the most desirable but also the most real avoids both intellectual and empirical issues and can be morally coercive. It can be criticised for the following reasons:

(i) The dysfunctions of the conventional family are not given adequate consideration and there is a failure to direct attention to the potentials for physical and psychological harm in 'ordinary' family life. Brown and his colleagues' studies of working-class women in an urban environment, for example, have identified depression as being associated with stressful life events, with economic difficulties, unemployment, overcrowding, housing and with the lack of a confiding relationship with one's husband (see Brown and Harris, 1978). Rapoport *et al.* (1977) have pointed out that while there is a statistical tendency for these factors to be associated with the less educated and less economically privileged social class groups, the relationship is only partial, and studies in all industrial nations have indicated that women from all social classes show a greater tendency than men to express dissatisfaction with themselves, their marriages and with life itself. Moore (1969) has also been sceptical about the actual nuclear family and has said that American social scientists were 'doing little more than projecting certain middle-class hopes and ideals onto a refractory reality'. While one can, in turn, be sceptical about his prophecy that there would be a qualitative transformation of the family into a system of 'mechanised and bureaucratised child-rearing', it is not difficult to see that, as he says, conditions have arisen which can prevent the family from performing the social and psychological functions ascribed to it by some sociologists.

(ii) The conventional model of the family disregards the diversity of family life. Diversity is now part of the social topography, and indeed it can be argued that there always has been a great variation in actual family life. But in a society where the nuclear family is considered to be the norm and the ideal, conformity is rewarded by conferring legal, social and economic advantages of status on marriage. For instance, only the married are licensed to be parents in both civil and ecclesiastical law and those who seek to remove the stigma of illegitimate birth are confronted by a web of legislation in addition to cultural attitudes and expectations. Ferri (1976) has pointed out that any deviation from the two-parent nuclear family 'makes it an obvious target for attack as a causal factor in numerous social and psychological ills and often the search for explanatory factors goes no further'. Deviation is punished and, for example, alternative forms of heterosexual cohabitation are negatively evaluated and sometimes negatively sanctioned. Various consequences for individuals, parents and children, flow from this perspective on family variance. Social disadvantages are marked by stigma and exclusion, and economic disadvantages by discrimination in taxation rates or in access to social security benefits. Literature on the family is full of concern about the social problems of broken homes, cohabiting parents, step-families and even of families where the mother goes out to work. Such labelling derives from what are essentially sociological and political assumptions about the way society should work, and are based on what Ryan (1971) has termed a victim-blaming ideology. Illegitimacy and divorce are thus both examples of stigmatised statuses (see Pinchbeck, 1954; Goode, 1964; Schlesinger, 1966,

1969; Marsden, 1973). It has been argued that, in part, this has occurred because people who live in 'atypical' family situations, such as single parents with children, or extended rather than nuclear families, do not make out a case for them in principle. However, the commune movement has been cited as helping to 'move family preferences out of the realm of pathology and deviance and into the realm of value and choice', and as helping 'to bring about a recognition of the possibility of diversity in family life and to legitimate experimentation in family forms' (Skolnick, 1973).

(iii) The conventional nuclear model implies a conservative attitude to change in the family system. Although it has been argued that the nuclear family is functionally necessary as part of a balanced social system, the traditionalists have failed to accept change in the family as a natural consequence to dysfunctional aspects of their utopian model. Any change has been regarded as problematic and it has been thought best that it did not happen. But, despite this, the idealist and sentimental view of the family does allow for some changes. The normal family is thought of as passing through a number of stages: marriage, child-bearing, child-rearing, dispersion, middle-life and retirement (Turner, 1969). The family life cycle is a concept used by family sociologists as well as being a lay concept, and is undoubtedly a useful approach to the study of the family. But it is not a description of how the nuclear family actually progresses or should progress. Although the concept implies change and adjustment over time, in that, for example, the family tasks and the relationships change (as does the household composition), and although such changes involve stress, the emphasis is upon the predictability and normality of these changes and of their taking place within the framework of the nuclear family itself. The problem associated with the concept of the life cycle is that it can have the effect of blinding us to the fact that a high proportion of families do not follow the standard cycle (30 to 35 per cent according to Turner).

It can also be morally coercive in that those who do not follow the cycle (that is, those who do not marry, or remain childless, or divorce) are considered deviant. This is hardly surprising, given that most societies have a high regard for marriage and marital stability. Marriage is seen as normal and desirable, and statistics such as the 1971 Census, which showed that 88 per cent of all those aged 30–49 were married, bear this out. Marriage is also seen as the moral accompaniment of maturity, when one supposedly stops the irresponsibility and immature behaviour of adolescence (Bell, 1972). Hence, the majority of people marry, have children, and stay married even if it requires accepting inconvenience and unpleasantness, as they have vested their identities in their marital status (Bell, 1972).

Even when there is divorce social pressure is exerted to encourage people to remarry (Goode, 1964). The institutional blockages facing divorced mothers in adjusting to a single status are particularly great, and although some remain single for a number of years (Ferri, 1976), the pressures are for them to re-enter the married state so as to conform once again to the accepted patterns and thereby reinforce them. The same is also true where divorced fathers have the care of their children (see George and Wilding, 1972). This conservative attitude to change tends to regard individual families and the family system as a relatively static institution. It does not raise questions such as 'How normal is normal?' Nor does it ask 'What is actually going on?' There is a failure to grasp the significance of the massive social and demographic changes associated with marriage, birth and divorce which have taken place during this century.

Demographic changes

Throughout the twentieth century there have been dramatic changes in the patterns of marriages, births, divorces and deaths, with far-reaching social implications for society and for individual families. 'Social commentators have referred to the silent revolution in marriage habits in the last two generations' (Finer Report, DHSS, 1974). The popularity and the early age of marriage was noted by Titmuss (1958) and the trend has continued, although there have been signs of levelling off (Fletcher, 1962; Young and Willmott, 1973; Chester, 1976a).

At the same time recent research and the publication of the Finer Committee's report on one-parent families have shown that the incidence of marriage breakdown in this country and in other western countries 'has become a major social phenomenon and one which is unlikely to go away' (Chester, 1976b). Divorce figures clearly demonstrate that more people are resorting to divorce to terminate marriages which have failed to live up to the ideals of romantic love and companionship. Whether or not the divorce figures indicate more marriage breakdown is not so clear, and it is important to recognise that high divorce rates are not incompatible with a belief in the fundamental stability of the family as a system. What they do suggest is a considerable fluidity in the composition of families within this system.

Demographic changes in recent years show quite clearly that the family is not a static institution. While the small nuclear family based on life-long, monogamous marriage may still be the norm, many individual families do not follow the standard life cycle. For some, marriages are not made yet children are born; such children, throughout their formative years, can experience a stable family situation with natural parents who may or may not marry after the birth, or can find themselves living in one or a combination of a number of 'anomalous' family situations. Similarly, legitimate children born into two-parent families can also experience changes in their family; the most common, as it usually precedes remarriage, is that of living in a one-parent family as a result of death, separation or divorce. It is not known how long children are likely to live in one-parent family situations, but for many it will not be a permanent situation, because they then become members of step-families.

Alongside changes in the marital status of families there has been a continuing fall in the number of children in families, which has had an impact on feminine life chances and has been described as 'one of the dominating biological facts of the twentieth century which has far reaching implications for the social position of women' (Titmuss, 1958). In his studies of families in Aberdeen, Gill (1977) has shown that the trend from a five- or six- towards a one- or two-child family appears to be firmly established. The steady fall in the birthrate between 1964 and 1978 (CSO, 1978) suggests that small families have become the norm, although predictions based on short-term trends have proved in the past to be unreliable. One result of the decline in the birthrate has been that illegitimate births as a proportion of all births have increased (Hartley, 1975; Gill, 1977).

Various explanations have been proffered to account for these far-reaching changes. The Finer Report (DHSS, 1974), which is as much a comment on contemporary marriage as it is on one-parent families, summarises the key associated factors which have accompanied change in marriage habits and fertility as (1) the changing situation and status of women, (2) the weakening of the authority of religion, (3) two world wars, which brought social and economic upheavals that provided circumstances favourable to change, and (4) the twentieth-century stance, which emphasises the welfare and happiness of individuals. Chester (1971) recognised such factors and has said that 'it begins to seem probable that changes in social conditions developing throughout the post-war period are now being reflected in the statistics of various kinds of personal behaviour and there have been changes in the norms of marriage'.

Changes in family patterns are not necessarily either happy or unhappy facts. There is, however, a tendency among social commentators and the lay public to equate change with deterioration. The Finer Report (DHSS, 1974) has suggested that it is 'unhistorical and socially unrealistic' to interpret marriage breakdown 'merely or exclusively as a concern of social pathology'. During the late 1950s and the early 1960s, for example, a debate raged about the state of health of the modern family. On one side were the moral pessimists, who decried what they considered to be the decline of the family, and on the other side sociologists, such as Fletcher (1962), who argued strongly against the prevailing gloom and accusations of moral degeneration. Fletcher's polemical defence of the modern family rejected the charges that the family had declined and that parental responsibility had deteriorated. Although the incidence of divorce and reasons for seeking such decrees changed dramatically during the late 1960s and early 1970s, partly as a result of the Divorce Reform Act 1969, Fletcher's argument remains valid. However, the kind of debate which took place in the 1960s, although interesting, is not very useful for social policy makers and practitioners and can, indeed, be harmful unless it also contains a well-informed understanding of social change, and an evaluation of the far-reaching implications of such change for the functioning of the family.

Social attitudes

To argue for the recognition of the dynamic nature of the family is not to overlook the fact that the changes that have taken place in recent years, such as the rise in rates of illegitimacy and the greater propensity to divorce, pose many problems for society, for the individual families, and quite specifically the children concerned, who experience the various crises. But society has to come to terms with the changes in marriage habits and make the appropriate response in terms of social policy.

Negative consequences flow from labelling those families which depart from the conventional model of the family as deviant. Sprey (1969), for instance, has pointed out that it is not a great leap from a status which occurs infrequently, and often ambiguously, to a socially stigmatised one, and Skolnick (1973) writes that 'the assumption that one form of the family is not only the most desirable, but also the most real and observable form . . . dictates social policies that stigmatize certain family and sexual behaviours as pathological deviance'. Attitudes to illegitimacy and one-parent families, and, to a lesser extent, to step-families and adopted families, provide examples of this process.

Becker's work on deviance and 'outsiders' is relevant here; his concern is with the process by which individuals come to be thought of as outsiders and their reactions to that judgement:

> All social groups make rules and attempt at some times and under some circumstances to enforce them. Social rules define situations and the kinds of behaviour appropriate to them, specifying some actions as 'right', and forbidding others as 'wrong'. When a rule is enforced, the person who is supposed to have broken it may be seen as a special kind of person, one who cannot be trusted to live by the rules agreed on by the group. He is regarded as an outsider (Becker, 1960).

A sociological view of deviance focuses on a failure to obey group rules, but there is a problem in deciding which rules are to be taken as the yardstick against which behaviour is measured and judged deviant. As Becker (1960) points out, 'deviance is not a simple quality, present in some kinds of behaviour and absent in others . . . The same behaviour may be an infraction of the rules at one time, and not at another . . .' The central fact about deviance is that it is created by society and is 'not a quality of the act the person commits, but rather a consequence of the application by others of rules and sanctions to an "offender"'. Moreover, the degree to which other people will respond to a given act as deviant varies greatly.

There can be variation over time, and variation according to who commits the act and who is injured, and some rules are enforced only when they result in certain consequences; here the unmarried mother furnishes a clear example. Vincent (1961) has shown that illicit sexual relations seldom result in censure or sanctions, unless they break taboos such as incest or extreme youth. But if a girl becomes pregnant as a result of extramarital sexual activity, the reaction of others is likely to be severe, at least on mothers if not on fathers, even in this so-called permissive age. Where illegitimate births occur, the unwed mother may be regarded as having broken the rules and, by some, as being a social problem.

It is important to recognise that 'anomalous' families, such as those where there is a lone parent or a step-parent, or where the children are illegitimate, are not in themselves a problem. For example, it is not illegitimate birth that causes children to be disadvantaged; rather it is the definition or meaning that society gives to that birth status, which defines the child's position and access to resources and which then poses problems for society, for the mother, and for the child.

As Kriesberg (1970) has stated, 'many of the difficulties faced by the mothers and children in female headed families are not inherent to that family structure'. They stem, in part, from the expectations of others about what is a normal family. Sprey (1969), too, has pointed out that 'the absence of a father can be aggravated, decreased or neutralized due to the effects of other conditions such as the availability of funds, relatives and community services'. In looking at the effects of English divorce law in the context of European trends, Chester (1976b) has written: 'Clearly it is important for us to begin to understand that many problems currently associated with one-parent families are not entailed in this condition, but stem from anachronistic attitudes and policies, some of them flowing from a misunderstanding of the ways in which our family system is changing in unison with others in the western world.'

Norms can be taken as read and no thought given to the manner in which the norms themselves contribute to the development of the problem (Ryan, 1971). For example, in a society where the two-parent family is the norm and where the family gains economic support from the male head of the household by means of wages, the absence of a husband generally means poverty unless income-maintenance schemes provide a viable alternative. Living in family units which do not conform to the norm, and which are negatively sanctioned by moralistic overtones, can have an effect on the children, as the inferior status of the family can rub off on to them, so

that they come to be regarded as inferior too (Davis, 1948).
Society is not usually prepared to accept that it can actually cause the problems through, for example, stigma, legal disabilities and poverty. Rather the cause is attributed to the person, who is regarded as problematic, and it is thought that there would be no problem if there was no deviation; in a sense, of course, this is true. However, the negative evaluation of families which depart from the traditional model goes beyond stigma. Families which do not conform to the norm are often regarded as being dysfunctional, particularly in relation to parenting, child-care and socialisation. For example, it is often assumed that only small families, with the traditional division of labour, and with the wife in full-time mothering, can adequately carry out the parental task. Some of the literature suggests that working mothers, lone parents or step-parents cannot adequately perform the roles which society expects, and such views persist despite conflicting evidence (Yudkin and Holme, 1963; Fogarty *et al.*, 1971; Maddox, 1975; Ferri, 1976; Rutter and Madge, 1976; Pilling and Pringle, 1978).

There is also a tendency to be preoccupied with form rather than with function. For instance, there has been a preoccupation with father-absence rather than an examination of the role of the father and the extent to which that role is adequately performed in 'intact' families (Pilling and Pringle, 1978). Another example of this preoccupation is the 'principle of legitimacy' (Malinowski, 1964). It is recognised that the form this principle assumes varies, yet it is assumed by proponents that the father is necessary for the sociological as well as the legal status of the child and its mother, and that a family group consisting of a woman and her offspring is incomplete and therefore illegitimate. Harris (1969) has pointed out that 'placement within a society is always necessary, but there is no need for it to depend on the recognition of parentage. As long as parentage is recognised, however, and parents given charge over their children in their most formative years, it is highly unlikely that an individual's parentage will not constitute one of the dimensions on which he is placed'.

It is not intended to argue that there are no associations between family situation and child development. Research on 'anomalous families' and child development suggests that family situation does matter. For instance, there is considerable evidence to show that in our society the lives of children from 'incomplete' or 'broken' families are adversely affected by a combination of circumstances – not only in emotional but also in social and educational development (e.g. Lewis, 1954; Wynn, 1964; Pringle, 1971; West and Farrington, 1973; Ferri, 1976). Children from large families form another group which has been found to be suffering from considerable disadvantage at school (see Douglas, 1964; Nisbet and Entwistle, 1967; Fogelman, 1975). But it must be noted that, in practice, children from large families tend to be found more frequently in lower social class groups and so they may be disadvantaged in many other ways. Once again we are faced with the question of whether difficulty and disadvantage are inherent in the family structure or whether they are related to factors such as low social class, low income and poor housing, which tend to be associated with families, such as one-parent families, that depart from the conventional model.

A rigid view of the nuclear family, particularly when that amounts to idealisation, can have serious consequences for some families and some children. It could be argued that the view that only the two-child, two-parent family is viable and desirable is anti-democratic. The idealisation of the conventional family militates against a conception of family life as having many possible forms, and, hence, there is little scope or approval for people to choose and stretch their experience in new ways, or to create satisfactory solutions for themselves and their children, and to achieve legitimate family goals.

In view of the demographic changes which have taken place during this century the conventional nuclear family is clearly one variant rather than the model of the family by which all other types of families are judged, although it is likely to continue as the major pattern. As Rapoport *et al.* (1977) have written, 'there is a sense in which variation, either by chance or by choice is now the norm' and 'there are changes under way that make the gap between the myth of the idealized nuclear family and the reality even more apparent'. Cooper (1974) has said that 'these changes may be seen either as an eroding of or simply a re-alignment of family functions and roles; but society must still provide for child-bearing and child-rearing to secure the continuity of social and individual identity or jeopardize its future'. Once a change of attitude has taken place towards 'anomalous' families, it will become easier for those family members to adapt and to operate. At the moment such families tend to get insufficient attention and an insufficient share of the resources.

4

Illegitimacy

The labelling of illegitimacy as a social problem is applied not only by the layman and the social work professionals. Attention has been drawn to the different approaches to the study of illegitimacy as long ago as 1939 by Kingsley Davis, who identified two approaches, which he termed the 'social welfare' and 'sociological'. It was his view that the former had led to the study of illegitimacy as being 'a matter of morals and policy rather than scientific theory' and as such failed to take into account the institutional norms and attitudes which define certain births as illegitimate and which fix the status of the people concerned.

A review of the literature since 1939 relating to illegitimacy in fact identifies at least three broadly different approaches to the study. There is the sociological approach, which enquires into the norms, attitudes and function of illegitimacy (for example, Pinchbeck, 1954; Vincent, 1961; Malinowski, 1964; Goode, 1964; Ryan, 1971; Hartley, 1975; Gill, 1977). Some of the strands in this approach are historical, while others could almost be termed anthropological. Interwoven into both strands are the development of laws and customs in different countries and societies. A further element lies in the influence of moral and religious beliefs. Then there is the psychological approach, which looks at individuals for causal explanations (Young, 1954; Wimperis, 1960). The social welfare approach overlaps with the psychological to some extent, but is more problem-orientated (see Wynn, 1964; Roberts, 1966; Pochin, 1969; Holman, 1970b; Kriesberg, 1970; Crellin *et al.*, 1971; Marsden, 1973).

Illegitimacy is a problem to society because it requires two responses which essentially conflict. On the one hand there is the wish to uphold the cultural norms and yet, on the other, there is the necessity to define the status and placement of the child and to ensure some economic and social support. According to Davis (1939), 'people are not supposed to have illegitimate children, but when they do an emergency is set into operation to give the child a status, though an inferior one, and to define the position of the parents. In this way society continues'. It is this response, and the ascription to the child of an inferior status, which creates problems for the mother and child. From this flow various disabilities, legal and social, as reflected in the history of the poor law (see Pinchbeck, 1954; Middleton, 1971) and in twentieth-century income-maintenance schemes (George, 1974).

Present legislation and social attitudes can only be understood in the light of earlier attitudes. Up to the twentieth century Pinchbeck (1954) summarises the situation in Britain thus:

> . . . two separate trends.have in the main been responsible for the legal and social status of the illegitimate child. First, the medieval maxim 'filius nullius' which pushed to its logical conclusion in the courts, has discriminated against him in many of the statutory developments affecting the relations of parents and illegitimate child and, secondly, social discrimination which has resulted from dependence and from transferring to him in full the moral guilt of his parents. To do otherwise, it was believed, could only increase the number of illegitimate children.

By the twentieth century more liberal attitudes were beginning to develop, and there have been enlargements of the rights of illegitimate children, particularly in recent years (Gill, 1977). But it is worth noting that in British law the natural father still has very few rights and the illegitimate child derives his or her status from the mother, who is either unmarried or is, or has been, married to someone else. Even during this century demands for equality before the law for all children on the grounds of social justice have been invariably met with fears for the institution of marriage and fears that a greater equality would provoke an increase in illicit relationships and a rise in the illegitimate birthrate. In Scandinavia, and in Sweden in particular, there has been a general trend of progressive legislation, but English bastardy law still contains much of the old 'guilt obsession' and stigma of the poor law, and lags behind that of other countries. The present social system also reflects the values of the past in treating one group of one-parent families – namely, those broken by death –

preferentially, whereas a rational system based on the needs of family members would not provide benefits according to the reason why the family broke up, or was never together, but would treat all one-parent families as a group alike (George, 1974).

Malinowski (1964) has argued that there is a sociological law that every child must have a 'sociological father'. Motherhood is never allowed to remain a mere biological fact and the 'law' states that 'the most important moral and legal rule concerning the physiological side of kinship is that no child should be brought into the world without a man – and one man at that – assuming the role of sociological father, that is, guardian and protector, the male link between the child and the rest of the community'. According to this view, cultures and sub-cultures with high illegitimacy rates are considered to be sociologically deviant, and an understanding is necessary of the forces which have prevented these groups from conforming to the norm of legitimacy. Goode (1964), for example, denies the existence of counter-norms which support consensual unions or other forms of unwed motherhood. Instead he sees an explanation of the differences in illegitimacy rates among various social classes and ethnic sub-cultures in terms of anomie theories.

Others have held that, while the principle of legitimacy is universal, the phenomenon of illegitimacy is related not only to this principle but to closely related norms as well (Vincent, 1961). A society may hold negative sanctions against illegitimacy and, at the same time, maintain permissive norms about related sexual behaviour (Roberts, 1966). Cross-cultural patterns of illegitimacy have been compared by Hartley (1975), and while she found that structural explanations have some plausibility, she argued that none of them is universally adequate. Instead she constructed her 'Concatenated Theory of Illegitimacy'. Basically this contains an independent series of variables which can be viewed as determining illegitimacy directly, yet each one is influenced by environmental, structural and cultural forces.

A carefully documented study such as Hartley's is in direct contrast to the unchecked beliefs about illegitimacy which Ryan (1971) claims lead to 'victim-blaming' theories. These can be summarised as (1) there is a prevalence of promiscuity, particularly pre-marital, among the poor, (2) poor girls are not concerned about the consequences of sexual activities, (3) as a result of (1) and (2) they have a lot of illegitimate babies, (4) illegitimacy is more acceptable to the poor, and (5) this is because 'welfare' provides a simple and practical economic solution. Ryan refers to a study by Lewis (1959), who found that mothers accept their daughters, and their children, because they love them, but they do not value legitimacy any the less. Perhaps they value it more because they have more practical and realistic knowledge of the consequences of illegitimacy.

This view would not, however, accord with some of the psychological explanations of unwed motherhood, which hold that this is a sympton of emotional disturbance and must be explained psychodynamically (see Young, 1954). Such views are based on research done on the client populations of social work agencies or psychiatric clinics, and for this reason have often been criticised.

Illegitimacy has also been held to be 'functionally useful to society', and to eliminate it would be 'to eliminate the raw material of the adoption process' (Ryan, 1971). To some extent this is a simplistic view and has been made more so by recent trends in the availability of contraception and abortion, on the one hand, and by numbers of children in public or voluntary care, on the other.

Gill (1977), in his study of illegitimate births in Aberdeen, discusses the relevance of the changing status of women to patterns of sexual behaviour. This has also been related to wider changes in social and personal values and in personal behaviour which have been taking place in the post-war period (Chester, 1976a). It has already been noted in the previous chapter on the family that the fall in the birthrate has had a dramatic effect on the lives of women and has given them far more power of choice. Gill (1977) suggests that this has led to a gradual redefinition of the marital relationship to

. . . an emotional partnership from which either partner is justified in withdrawing if fulfilment is not achieved. Sanctions against extra-marital sexual relations are correspondingly weakened and this conception of marriage is most widely held in middle-class groups and in the larger urban centres. Laws relating to divorce are still somewhat restrictive, thus encouraging consensual unions and hence the birth, not merely of illegitimate children, but of illegitimate families.

This last point leads to the question of illegitimate children growing up. Gill's findings show that 'for illegitimate children the pathways in terms of care arrangements were from fatherlessness rather than towards it. Among legitimate children the pathways were the reverse – from a complete family unit to fatherlessness' (Gill, 1977). Only 11 out of 117 mothers of illegitimate children born between 1950 and 1955 who were followed up in 1964 had remained both unmarried and unsupported, and the majority of the illegitimate children were living in 'complete' families in 1964. Approximately 11 per cent of the legitimate children had had experience of family disruption since birth, and only a third of this 11 per cent were living in 'complete' families in 1964. Gill compared children living in single-parent units or in families with 'anomalous' backgrounds with those in 'complete' families and found that in several respects children (legitimate or illegitimate) living in single-parent units were at a disadvantage compared with their peers. Gill (and his colleagues) paid considerable attention to the question of social class. This was measured by the mother's pre-pregnancy or premarital occupation and also by her occupation in 1964. Single-parent families and those with anomalous backgrounds were found to have a very definite lower social class bias, but if the mothers returned to work, they were no more likely than mothers from 'complete' families to be downwardly socially mobile.

Bohman (1971) compared a group of illegitimate children in Sweden who had remained with their natural mothers with a group adopted at an early age and with a group who were adopted or fostered later in childhood. By the age of 11 approximately 30 per cent of the children who were living with their natural mother also had their own father living in the family, and the majority of children in all the groups were living with two parents or parent-substitutes rather than with a lone parent. Bohman studied the children's school adjustment and school marks in Swedish and maths. No significant differences in school adjustment were found for boys or girls when those in the three groups were compared, but there were differences in adjustment between boys from all three groups of illegitimate children and 'controls' selected from their classmates. The illegitimate boys and also girls in the group who had been adopted or fostered later in childhood were not so well adjusted as their legitimately born controls. Although children in the three illegitimate groups had lower average school marks than their classmate controls, it was mainly the group adopted or fostered late which did significantly worse, and Bohman suggests that this was associated with various forms of handicap found more frequently in this group.

Tizard (1977) followed a small group of illegitimate children who were all in residential care until at least the age of two and then some were placed for adoption or fostered, some were restored to their natural mothers and some remained in institutions. When the children were last tested at 8, those restored to their natural parents had lower IQs and school attainment than the adopted children, but this was related to social class. The school behaviour of both restored and adopted children was considered poor in comparison with that of various other groups. Tizard suggests that this may be related to the children's insatiable desire for attention and their difficulty in forming good peer-group relationships; she further suggests that these factors may be related to their early life experiences and institutional rearing, although there may be other genetic, biological or environmental explanations.

Numerous studies, in addition to those mentioned, refer to the importance of environmental factors when studying the circumstances of single-parent families (see Hunt *et al.*, 1973). Such families usually contain a proportion of illegitimate children even though, as has already been pointed out, the majority move into two-parent situations during the early years of childhood. Those who remain in (or come back into) single-parent families often tend to feel acutely the deprivations that arise out of the poor housing, low incomes, lack of day care facilities, loneliness and other difficulties in which many of them live. However, Ferri (1976) has suggested that illegitimate children in one-parent families may derive some benefit from experiencing a 'fairly stable, although materially disadvantaged, home environment' in comparison with the disruption and stress of a family broken by the separation of the parents. She found that illegitimate children living in fatherless families at the age of 11 showed 'few adverse effects due to their family situation as such, after allowance had been made for the handicaps associated with it'. The illegitimate children followed up by Ferri were part of the larger group of illegitimate children who were studied at 7 (Crellin *et al.*, 1971) and who are now the subjects of the present investigation of their characteristics and development by the age of 11.

5
Adoption

The kind of home an adopted child finds himself in, the material circumstances, and the attitudes of parents and relatives towards adoption, and to the particular adopted child, are all important to the development and happiness of that child. In many respects adoptive families are like other families in that they tend to contain two parents and conform to accepted family norms. But, like single-parent families, foster families, and other 'anomalous' families, they do have distinctive characteristics; in evolution they do not conform to the usual family life cycle and because of their special characteristics they should be considered as a variant from the conventional family.

The similarities and differences of adoptive families compared to non-adoptive families have been identified by Jaffee and Fanshel (1970), in a retrospective study of parents who adopted during the period 1930–1940. Adoptive families are like other families in that they are legally constituted with rights and responsibilities common to 'natural' families, they seek to meet all the major functions of the conventional family with respect to the needs of the adults and children, and after children arrive they experience broadly similar developmental processes to other families. But there are some differences, and in particular adoptive parents must contend with a problem of identity resolution parallel to that facing their child, who must experience and resolve complex identity problems. Adoptive parents 'need to develop a feeling of entitlement to their child' (Jaffee and Fanshel, 1970).

There have been few attempts to develop a theory about adoptive families, but Kirk (1964) provides an exception. He argues that there are special dynamics operating in the adoptive family which set it apart from the biological family. Although there are exceptions, childlessness is generally an involuntary condition in married people and places them in an anomalous position in a society which is pro-parenthood (Humphrey, 1969). The pressures towards parenthood are evident and have been well documented by family sociologists. Waller (1951) wrote of two conspiracies, one to get the single to marry and the other of parents to get the childless to have children. Pohlman (1970) too has noted this conspiracy: 'Family activities and family values are exalted in the popular media and in the design of homes, communities, and a variety of facilities.' He quotes Rainwater (1965), who identifies a central norm that 'one should not have more children than one can support, but one should have as many children as one can afford'. In Rainwater's study people who had large families were viewed as somewhat good and those with small families as less laudable, often as selfish. It is not surprising, therefore, that there are pressures (often internalised by prospective parents) to conform. Adoption, however, in many cases is a decision reached after many years of frustration and disappointment and may have followed unsuccessful treatment for infertility. In a study on 'the background of the quest for an adoptive child' (Child Adoption, 1975) prospective parents undergoing fertility treatment spoke of the stress associated with childlessness and of the trying pressures from family and friends. One is quoted as saying 'you get the feeling when they come to see you that they think it's your fault, you're not wanting children, that there's something odd about you . . .' Another is reported as saying 'this is what I've got more than anything, a tremendous sense of failure – towards my husband too – because it's me. Society has this pressure on you too, firstly to get married and then have children, especially if career-wise you're not going very far'.

Childless couples entering upon adoption are thus confronted with a series of difficulties which can be described as 'role handicap'. Kirk's theory states that this role handicap is reinforced by the attitudes of other people towards childlessness and adoption even after adoption has taken place (Kirk, 1964). It is possible, therefore, that parental dilemmas and stresses manifest themselves in the evolving family relationships. Adoptive parents, however, have ways of coping with such difficulties. According to Kirk, they either deny that their situation is different from that of biological parents or they acknowledge the difference.

In developing his views Kirk refers to Kurt Lewin's theories on minority group membership, seeing a relevance to the adoptive situation. In citing the minority group position of Jews, Lewin (1948) suggests that adoptive parents, likewise, make it a position of strength. Kirk does, however, see a dissimilarity, as Jewish parents originally share with the child characteristics on which the social stigma of minority group status is based. He argues that this interdependence is less readily given in adoption, where there is no longer a natural group beyond the family. He also points out that it is relatively rare for adoptive parents themselves to have been adopted. However, this interdependence is necessary, and Kirk argues that this 'shared fate' has to be developed. This is not easy and 'it would seem impossible for adoptive parents to create a real inter-dependence unless they can convincingly relate their own fate to the child's'.

One significance of viewing adoptive families as a minority group is that it is best that facts arising out of the adoption and events preceding it, such as illegitimate birth or childlessness, are faced squarely from the start and the child involved in the knowledge. Such awareness and openness can minimise ambiguity, tension and the possibility of maladjustment in the child as he or she grows up.

Telling about adoption related to successful outcome

The need to tell has been identified by researchers over many years (Brenner, 1951; Kirk, 1964; McWhinnie, 1967; Kornitzer, 1968; Lawder, 1970; Triseliotis, 1973). Moreover, it is generally considered important that children should learn of their adoptive status at an early age (Pringle, 1967). Yet it is well known that many adopters do not find this easy, and 'telling' is perceived as 'an act which sets in motion complex and emotion-laden wheels which change the family dynamics and which may create some problems for the growing child' (Rowe, 1970). This is borne out by the previous National Children's Bureau study, where, by the time the children were 9, some parents had done no more than mention the word 'adoption' and altogether one in five of adoptive parents, 'while paying lip service to the principle of "telling", had failed to put it into practice, some through inhibition and others through lack of understanding' (Seglow *et al.*, 1972). Only about half the children in the study were said by their parents to have accepted the fact of their adoption quite readily; one in twenty were reported anxious or confused about it; and one in four were said to have been uninterested (Seglow *et al.*, 1972). Tizard (1977) suggests that younger children often seem to resist adoption being talked about, as the information is difficult to make sense of and the child does not welcome knowing that he is different and his parents are not his own. Adolescents are usually more curious and may even welcome the knowledge that they have other parents, but at the same time they are likely to be much more resentful if the 'telling' is postponed altogether until adolescence. Without openness, adopted children may have difficulties in emotional adjustment, in some cases possibly leading to the need for psychiatric treatment. The adopted child has to integrate the knowledge that another set of parents, whom he does not know, procreated him and made a decision to relinquish him. Many of them have to come to terms with the knowledge that they were born illegitimately, and with the fact that their adoptive parents are not biologically related to them. Where they are biologically related to the adopters, an even greater sense of 'genealogical bewilderment' can arise.

This term was coined by Sants (1964) to refer to problems of personal identity which he found during clinical studies of adopted children referred with problems of maladjustment to child-guidance clinics, and which he identified as one factor in 'adoption stress'. According to Sants (1964) 'a genealogically bewildered child is one who either has no knowledge of his natural parents or only uncertain knowledge of them. The resulting state of confusion and uncertainty . . . fundamentally undermines his security and this affects his mental health'. He suggests that this condition can arise out of the failure of parents to share with the child their knowledge of his biological background and the circumstances surrounding his adoption.

Parental attitudes and circumstances related to adoption success

The view that the personal qualities of adoptive parents are of paramount importance for placements to be successful has been expressed by a number of authors. Jacka (1973), for example, typifies this by writing, 'the most certain thing that is known about the adoption process is that its "success" depends more than anything else on the adopting couple, and on their having the right attitude to children'. He suggests that the weight of evidence shows

. . . the positive association of successful and happy adoptions judged over short periods and long periods with such things as a warm and accepting attitude on the part of the adopters to children; a recognition and acceptance by the adopters of the adopting role; a warm, stable adopting family; a sensible and understanding attitude to infertility, illegitimacy and the natural parents on the part of the adopting parents themselves, and their relatives, particularly the grandparents.

Others have said that 'parental attitudes' are more important in relation to the development of adopted children than such factors as social class. McWhinnie (1967), for instance, concludes that the adoption outcome is more dependent on parental attitudes than on any other variable. Tizard (1977) found mutual attachment between parent and child was related to parental satisfaction with adoption.

There can be no doubt that 'warm and accepting attitudes' are important to the happiness of any child. Acceptance of the adopted child and his background by his adoptive parents can help to overcome identity problems which may arise, and is particularly important in relation to the adopted child's security and propensity to learn. A difficulty in research, however, is to define in precise and measurable terms exactly what are the right attitudes (Jacka, 1973). So, while on commonsense grounds attitudes can be considered important for the outcome of adoption, it is important not to overstate their significance without precise definition and measurement. Because of such methodological difficulties it is not known that parental attitudes are more important than other factors. Moreover, it is difficult to know because attitudes, motivations, and expectations are all related to social class (see Chapter 2).

In two comparative studies concerned with the development of adopted children (Bohman, 1970; Seglow *et al.*, 1972) there was no measurement of 'warm and accepting attitudes', although the researcher who interviewed the adoptive parents of the children in the National Child Development Study when the children were $8\frac{1}{2}$ to 9 made some attempt to assess the parents' attitudes and interest in their adopted child. About half the mothers were considered to have a warm and positive attitude towards their child and the majority of fathers were said to be interested in their adopted child. There was also an attempt to assess the teacher's perception of parental interest in the children's education and schooling, but teachers' perceptions of parental concern are known to be subjective and selective (see Banfield *et al.*, 1966; Pritchard and Butler 1975).

Of course, adoptive parents, like other parents, may hold some attitudes which are not always favourable to their child's well-being. For example, Mandell (1973) has pointed out that adoptive parents have been noted to have high aspirations, which can induce stress in a child. Seglow *et al.* (1972) found a high proportion of adoptive mothers were over-concerned with education, but Tizard (1977) in her study noted 'little evidence of undue pressure on the children for academic achievement'. However, she does refer to a generally high level of joint parent–child activity in the adoptive families, and the fact that the majority of the parents regularly helped their children with school work. Such activities indicate a child-centred approach which may be linked with the middle-class background of many of the families. Thus even where parental attitudes can be identified, they cannot be set apart from environmental factors because they tend to mirror them.

A striking fact about adoption is that often a class transfer has taken place. Many children born to working-class mothers are subsequently brought up in middle-class families (Bohman, 1970; Seglow *et al.*, 1972; Grey and Blunden, 1971; Tizard, 1977). Children born to middle-class mothers more frequently continue to be brought up in adoptive homes of similar background. There is, however, some evidence that adopted children living in working-class homes do better than expected (Kadushin, 1970; Bohman, 1970; Seglow *et al.*, 1972). This suggests that there may be factors, which are usually class-related, associated with adoption. It may be that it is not adoption *per se* which is good for children but, rather, the combination of factors associated with it.

Social class, for instance, is usually a good indicator of material circumstances, but a number of studies have noted that most adopted children, whatever their social class background, were living in materially comfortable homes. To some extent this may be due to selection processes, which require prospective adopters to demonstrate a degree of financial security. It may also be due to the fact that adoptive parents tend to be older than natural parents and, therefore, more likely to be settled in their jobs and in their homes. A significant factor may also be family size. The families of adopted children tend to be small, with the majority in two-child families and a considerable number being one-child families (Seglow *et al.*, 1972; Tizard, 1977).

A number of studies have suggested that children from poor and adverse backgrounds tend to do better than might be expected if they are given the advantage of a home whose material standards and standards of parental care are good or above average (Clarke and Clarke, 1974, 1976; Tizard, 1977). In what is regarded as a classic study Skeels and his colleagues investigated the mental development of a group of children from homes where the mothers had been classified as mentally retarded and/or where fathers were of low occupational status (Skeels and Harms, 1948). The children were placed, before the age of two years, in foster or adoptive homes which were selected as average for their adequate adjustment in the community. These children appeared to have benefited from being placed in a more favourable environment compared to that in which they were born, in that they attained a mental level which equalled that of the population as a whole. In another study Kadushin (1970) has described how some working-class children living with multi-problem families in slum conditions were transferred to middle-class homes. The 'success' rate of these children compared well with that of children in other adoption studies despite their very poor early upbringing.

While not disputing that the reversal of early adverse circumstances is possible, Rutter (1974) has shown that the evidence needs to be examined carefully. For instance, he has questioned whether the adopted children in the National Child Development Study were really disadvantaged at birth and whether the findings of this study when the children were 7 'point so clearly in the direction the authors say that they do'. The authors (Seglow *et al.,* 1972) regarded the adopted children, the majority of whom were born illegitimate, as having been 'born at risk', and considered that their favourable environment after adoption compensated for a bad start in life. Rutter (1974) agrees that, at the age of 7, the adopted children were generally faring well, but argued that on the basis of initial predictors they turned out about average. The indicators he examined included social class, birth order, number of younger siblings, sex of child and birthweight, and he concluded that, on the most important predictors of attainment (or adjustment), the adopted children started with an advantage, and on a larger number of minor predictors they started with a disadvantage. He acknowledged that the data were not available to balance the two, but considered that, as far as could be judged, 'they probably about even out'.

Sex of child related to parental satisfaction with adoption

Not all adoptions turn out well, and some parents express doubts about adoption (Brenner, 1951; Seglow *et al.*, 1972; Tizard, 1977). In the previous National Children's Bureau study, for instance, parents of 22 per cent of the 8- to 9-year-olds expressed doubts about the adoption, and dissatisfaction seemed more likely to occur when the child was a boy (Seglow *et al.*, 1972). It was thought that 'this could well be a reflection of feelings about bringing up boys or girls generally rather than about difficulties specific to the adoptive parents and their children' (Seglow *et al.*, 1972). However, it may have been the case that doubts about the outcome of the adoption were related to the preference parents had regarding the sex of their adopted child. Some parents may have adopted a boy against their preference, owing to the availability of children for adoption at the time or to agency placement practice, such as suggesting that adoptive parents have a boy first or children of each sex.

When the main reasons why the adopted children were relinquished by their mothers were examined (Seglow *et al.*, 1972), there was no clear evidence that the child's sex was a reason for relinquishment, although it may have been true that some mothers thought girls were easier to bring up single-handed, or that a male child would remind them of the putative father when they wished to forget him. However, the fact that a higher proportion of boys than girls were placed for adoption may, indeed, have meant that some adoptive parents had to modify their preferences.

A number of studies have shown that adoptive parents (particularly husbands) prefer to adopt girls rather than boys (Leahy, 1933; Brenner, 1951; Jaffee and Fanshel, 1970; Kirk, 1964; Bohman, 1970). Bohman (1970), for instance, found that almost half the adoptive mothers expressed a clear sex preference and two-thirds of them wanted to adopt a girl. He also found that preferences related to the cause of childlessness. While noting that any conclusions must be tentative, he stated, 'there does seem to be a tendency for the reluctance to adopt a boy to be most pronounced in the marriages where infertility was due to the husband. The wives appear to have had a more definite preference for girls when they themselves were the cause of the infertility . . .' Kirk (1964), too, found that girls are favoured by adopters, and he argues that adoptive fathers may be reluctant to adopt male children because of the importance placed in western society upon continuity of the family line. For most people inheritance is not an issue, but it may be that kinship sentiments (patrilineality) may exist. Brenner (1951) also noted that the preference for a girl might arise from the couple's fear that the adopted child could not fully become a member of their family. It has been argued that women suffer most from childlessness, and Kirk (1964) suggests that in adoption they may be prepared to compromise their preference for a boy by stating a preference for a girl in order to accommodate their husbands' reservations. Some have suggested, but without any real evidence, that a wife's desire for a girl child represents a narcissistic preference.

Boys placed in a family where a girl child is preferred may be exposed to ambivalent attitudes and behaviour. If this is the case, the ambivalence may affect the development of the child. For example, Bohman (1970) found that, although the relationship was not statistically significant, there was a tendency for adjustment to be better among the boys where adoptive mothers openly declared a preference for a boy, and he concluded that 'the risk of maladjustment among the boys is greater if the mother desired a girl but received a boy'. Jaffee and Fanshel (1970) also found that 'in general the parents whose adopted children had fared best in their life adjustment had showed a greater tendency to be specific about the sex of the child they had wanted than had been true of the parents of adoptees with the most problematic adjustments'.

Sex of child as an influence on the outcome of adoption

The evidence concerning sex and the development of adopted children is sparse and inconclusive; the interpretative significance of sex differences is also far from clear. There is a need to compare adopted children with other children, as differences may be common to all children rather than being a feature of adoptive status. For instance, most interest has focused on sex differences in the adjustment of adopted children, and the general conclusion is that adopted boys are rated as less well adjusted than girls; but in this respect they are similar to boys in the general population (Davie *et al.*, 1972). It is also an open question whether the differences are real or whether they can be accounted for by different modes of adjustment, patterns of upbringing, or by artefacts of the measurement process, such as biases in teachers' ratings (see Nash, 1973).

Weinstein and Geisel (1960) found that differences favoured girls and that the two largest differences occur on measures for which conformity and control of aggression are important components. Nevertheless, the authors recognised that differences may have reflected normal socialisation into masculine roles not recognised by the measures used. Nemovicher (1959), although not studying sex differences among adopted children, found that adoption was the only factor accounting for differences in personality traits between a small group of adopted and non-adopted boys. The adopted boys were found to possess the traits of hostility, tenseness, dependency and fearfulness to a greater extent than non-adopted boys. This finding is supported by Bohman (1970), who found that maladjustment was somewhat more frequent among adopted boys than among schoolboys in general, and that adopted girls also displayed disturbances more frequently than schoolgirls in general, although the differences were less pronounced than in the case of adopted boys.

The earlier work of the National Child Development Study which compares adopted children with non-adopted children found that there was some indication that adopted boys were more often mentioned as having problems than other boys, while adopted girls were mentioned least of all (Seglow *et al.*, 1972). With regard to maladjustment, no difference was found between adopted children and the rest of the cohort, but a higher proportion of adopted boys were found to be 'maladjusted' when compared with all the boys in the study, whereas adopted girls showed a slightly lower proportion of maladjustment than the cohort. An interesting finding, and worthy of further explanation, was that adopted boys from middle-class homes showed a higher prevalence of maladjustment than non-adopted boys living in middle-class homes.

The present study provides the opportunity for a further examination of sex differences as one factor in the development of this same group of children by the age of 11. Hard evidence about such factors as parental attitudes may be lacking, but the association of other important environmental factors in the home with children's development will be considered. Particular attention will be paid to the family situation at 11 of adopted children in comparison with that of illegitimate and legitimate children who were not adopted.

Part II

The Children at 11: their Families and Environments

6

The Follow-up Study

The findings of this study of illegitimate and adopted children at the age of 11 come from data gathered for the National Child Development Study (NCDS). This is a follow-up study of approximately 16 000 children born in the week 3–9 March 1958 and living in England, Wales and Scotland. Originally information was collected on these children as part of the Perinatal Mortality Survey (Butler and Bonham, 1963). The children have now been followed up at the ages of 7 (see Davie *et al.*, 1972), 11 (see Wedge, 1969) and 16 (see Fogelman, 1976), and it is hoped to continue to study them as adults.

At each follow-up information has been collected from several different sources about various aspects of the children's background and development. Firstly, a parental interview was carried out by a health visitor, usually with the child's mother or mother-substitute, sometimes with the father, or in other cases with a caring adult. This provided details about the child's home environment and the composition of the family, and information related to the child's progress and development. Secondly, an educational questionnaire completed by the child's teachers provided details about the school and the child's progress in school. Thirdly, the children themselves completed a series of ability and attainment tests and answered some individual questions. Fourthly, the school medical officers examined the children and recorded details of their physical development and medical history.

The measures used in this report will be described in detail in the relevant chapters and sections. Further information can be gained by referring to the books mentioned or to the many additional books and papers arising from the National Child Development Study. In particular, the two books on these same groups of children (Crellin *et al.*, 1971; Seglow *et al.*, 1972) cover at the earlier age of 7 many of the same aspects as those in the present report.

The sample at 11

Following up earlier studies is not always a simple matter. First, there are likely to be changes in the sample, owing to events such as death or emigration, difficulties in retracing families and refusals to participate. Such changes can, however, be enumerated and the extent of any resulting biases calculated. Secondly, decisions have to be taken about following up particular groups, if these have varied.

In the earlier study of the adopted children (Seglow *et al.*, 1972) there were potentially three sub-groups, although one sub-group (those adopted by an own parent) was excluded. The other two sub-groups were those who were born illegitimate and later adopted, and those who were legitimately born and later adopted. Some of the analyses combined these two sub-groups into one adopted group (which was then redivided according to factors within the adoption situation itself, such as agency or non-agency placements). These adopted children were the subjects of an additional 'intensive follow-up' study when aged $8\frac{1}{2}$ to $9\frac{1}{2}$, although, for various reasons, some of the families did not take part (Seglow *et al.*, 1972). At other times in the report the sub-group of children born illegitimate and later adopted were compared with the illegitimate children who had not been adopted, and with legitimate (not adopted) children. These latter three groups were also compared in the parallel study of illegitimate children (Crellin *et al.*, 1971).

The present study is essentially a follow-up of the children who were born illegitimate, and seeks to describe and compare the situation at 11 of children who, at 7, had been grouped into the following three legitimacy status groups:

(1) illegitimate, not adopted (but *including* illegitimate children adopted by one of their own parents);
(2) illegitimate adopted;
(3) legitimate (not adopted).

Thus the present study will have much to report about a particular group of adopted children, but will not consider the total range of adoption experience.

A third set of decisions concerned the longitudinal aspects. It would have been possible to include children who had come back into the study by 11 after not taking part at the age of 7, or children who came into the study for the first time after the age of 7 (i.e. immigrants), or to regroup children whose status had changed (for example, those children adopted between the ages of 7 and 11, of whom there were only known to be three). However, the longitudinal nature of the follow-up requires that the same groups of children are studied at 11 as at 7.

The findings reported in this book use data from the Perinatal Mortality Survey and the National Child Development Study which were gathered in the course of following up all the children in the study. Compared with the two earlier reports (Crellin *et al.*, 1971; Seglow *et al.*, 1972) the range of topics has been somewhat reduced in order to focus on certain key issues concerning the situation at the age of 11 of children who were born illegitimate, in respect of their family situation and home background, their physical development and their social adjustment and attainment at school.

Numbers in the groups at 11

At the time of the 7-year follow-up in 1965 there were 366 children in the illegitimate sample and 182 in the adopted sample (Crellin *et al.*, 1971, p. 57, and Table A8.1). Since then two further follow-ups have taken place, in 1969 and 1974, and during this time a great deal of work was done on checking records and correcting mistakes. For this reason the total number of illegitimate children in the 7-year follow-up whom it would have been possible to retrace at 11 has been revised to 363, and the number of adopted children has been revised to 180 (Table A6.1).

Table 6.1 gives the sample at 11: 294 illegitimate children, 115 adopted children, 12 076 legitimate children. The table shows the number of deaths and emigrations which took place between the 7- and the 11-year-old follow-ups, and also the numbers who refused to take part at 11, or who were untraced or for whom no data were available on their parental situation and home background. As there was a comparatively low response rate at 11 for the adopted children (68 per cent), we explored possible biases in the 11-year adopted sample. The 7-year-old characteristics of the adopted children with

TABLE 6.1   *The sample at 11*

Legitimacy status	Total sample	Deaths	Emigrants	Sample excluding deaths/ emigrants (N = 100 %)	Refusals	Untraced/no parental data	Total with parental information
Illegitimate	363	0	7	356	15 (4.2 %)	47 (12.9 %)	294 (82.9 %)
Adopted	180	1	9	170	24 (14.1 %)	31 (18.2 %)	115 (67.7 %)
Legitimate	14 337	14	283	14 040	653 (4.7 %)	1 311 (9.3 %)	12 076 (86.0 %)

11-year parental information were compared with those of adopted children without parental information at 11.

First, the social class distribution was examined and no significant difference found (Table S6.1). Then the children's reading and arithmetic test scores, their social adjustment score and their height were looked at for each social class (Table S6.2). The only significant difference between adopted children included in the sample at 11 and those who were not was that the children from manual social class backgrounds included in the sample at 11 were taller at 7 than those not included. This difference will be referred to in the analysis of height (Chapter 12). Otherwise our analysis shows that the findings reported in this study about the adopted children are not likely to be biased through non-response.

There are several possible reasons why 55 (just less than one-third) of the adopted children were lost to the study at 11. One may be that some parents were becoming tired of being asked to answer questions for the National Children's Bureau at rather frequent intervals. They had taken part in the 7-year-old follow-up, were approached 18 months later for the intensive interview follow-up and now they were being asked to take part in another round approximately two years later. It is possible that in some of these cases the adoption was not working out too well, or there were other family problems, and the adoptive parents did not with to disclose or discuss the situation. Another possibility (which may be linked with both the other reasons) is that the parents did not want to be identified as 'adoptive' parents. Kirk (1964) has discussed the desire for normality which can lead some families to wish to 'forget' the fact of adoption, sometimes to the extent of not telling the child. In a few extreme cases there may have been a fear that the 11-year-old child might find out about his or her adoption through taking part in the study, and in other cases a fear that the child might somehow become unsettled by being singled out in this way.

7

Parental Care Situation

The expectation that children will be looked after by their own parents cannot be fulfilled in every case, even straight after birth. Illness, incapacity, breaks in the family, or death can intervene at any time. Illegitimate children are particularly vulnerable, as their parents are not married to each other and there is often no recognisable family for them to join. Only about 20 per cent of the mothers of the illegitimately born children in the NCDS were cohabiting with their child's father or another man at the time of birth (Crellin *et al.*, 1971). Many of the rest of the children would have been with their mothers in Mother and Baby Homes or in the maternal grandparents' home, or else they would have been placed in nurseries or foster homes. By the age of 7, 73 per cent 'were living in some kind of two-parent family including those who had been adopted' (Crellin *et al.*, 1971). On the other hand 10 per cent of the legitimate children were no longer living with both their own parents at the age of 7.

We therefore looked to see what the family situation was at 11 and how much change there had been during the four years. Before describing the results, we have set out the definitions of family situation and parental care used in the present study.

Family situations: some definitions

At each follow-up of the NCDS children information was obtained as to whether the study child was normally cared for by his or her natural mother and father or by one or more parent-substitutes. The family situations in which the children were living were numerous. Ferri (1976), in her study of the children who were in one-parent families when they were 11 years old, found that each follow up 'revealed more than 30 different types of "anomalous" parental situation'. Some of these, such as step-parents, are fairly easily defined, but others depended on how the particular family saw them. The presence in the household of a grandfather, for example, did not necessarily mean that he was considered to be acting as a father figure if the child's natural father was no longer in the home for whatever reason. Key categories of parental care situation have therefore been defined. They are as follows:

(a) *Natural parents* are both the own, or biological, parents of the study child living together but not necessarily, in the case of illegitimate children, married to each other.
(b) *Step-parents* are one natural parent and one step or adoptive parent or cohabitee (if they were not the natural parent of the child).
(c) *Adoptive parents*, neither of whom is a natural parent of the child, who have legally adopted the study child and are living together.
(d) *Mother (natural) alone* with no one acting as father figure.
(e) *Father (natural) alone* with no one acting as mother figure.
(f) *'Other situations'*, including a natural parent and, say, grand-parent (acting as a parent figure), relatives, foster parents, single 'substitute' (including adoptive) parents, and residential care.

Although category (f) contains a number of two-parent or parent-substitute situations, the term *two-parent family* will only be used in relation to categories (a), (b) and (c). It should be noted, however, that this definition of two-parent family is broader than that in the one-parent family studies based on the cohort (Ferri, 1976; Essen and Lambert, 1977), which defines only 'both natural parents' as a two-parent family.

Family situation at 11

Table 7.1 shows the family situation at 11 for the three legitimacy status groups of children. As expected, the majority (74 per cent) of the 409 illegitimately born children were living in a two-parent family at eleven. This number includes the children who had subsequently been adopted, but when they are excluded, the pattern is still clear. Out of the 294 illegitimate children who had not been adopted, 194 were living in two-parent families (65 per cent). The proportion of

TABLE 7.1   *Family situation at 11*

Legitimacy status	Natural parents	Step-parents	Adoptive parents	Mother alone	Father alone	Other situations	Total = 100%	Not known
Illegitimate	122 (41%)	72 (24%)	0 (–)	58 (20%)	2 (1%)	40 (14%)	294	0
Adopted	0 (–)	0 (–)	107 (93%)	0 (–)	0 (–)	8 (7%)	115	0
Legitimate	11 004 (91%)	306 (3%)	3 (–)†	504 (4%)	84 (1%)	168 (1%)	12 069	7

† These children were adopted after the 7-year follow-up – 15 legitimate children who were adopted before 7 have been excluded as they were not in this group at 7.

Illeg/legit by natural parents/all other family situations $\chi^2 = 777.8$ (1df)***
Illeg/legit by mother alone/all other family situations $\chi^2 = 158.0$ (1df)***

NOTE: The stars in this and subsequent tables indicate levels of significance. See Appendix 1.

illegitimate children living with both their natural parents at 11 (41 per cent) was very similar to that at 7.

It is not possible to know whether this pattern is typical of the family situations of illegitimate children of this age in the general population. However, a study of 2511 children aged 9 to 14 years in Aberdeen found that at the time of interview 73 per cent of the illegitimately born children were living in a two-parent family situation of some kind and of these 34 per cent (25 per cent overall) were living with their natural parents (Gill, 1977), figures which are very similar to our own.

Changes in family situation between 7 and 11

Table 7.2 shows what proportions of children living in each family situation at 7 were living in the same situation at 11 or had changed to a different parental situation. Illegitimate children were three times more likely to experience a change in parental care during this period than either legitimate or adopted children. In the four years there was a change in family situation for 15 per cent of the illegitimate children compared with 5 per cent of the legitimate or the adopted children.

When the patterns of change were looked at more closely, they showed considerable differences between illegitimate and legitimate children. This is not surprising, as any change from the situation at birth for illegitimate children is away from living with their mother alone (although they can also go back to this situation) and for legitimate children is away from living with both natural parents. During the ensuing years further changes become possible for both groups as children change into or out of step-families and so on, but these changes may continue to go in different directions, depending on legitimacy status. For instance, even though similar proportions of the illegitimate (51 per cent) and legitimate (54 per cent) children whose family situation changed between 7 and 11 were living with a lone parent at 11, a higher proportion of illegitimate children had at 7 been living in 'other situations' and a higher proportion of legitimate children had at 7 been living in two-parent families (Table A7.1).

Illegitimate children who were living with both natural parents at the age of 7 were less likely than legitimate children still to be in this situation, but the proportion of illegitimate and legitimate children living with step-parents at the age of 7 who were still in the same situation at 11 was not significantly different (Table 7.2). Although 82

TABLE 7.2   *Family situation at 7 and 11*

(a) Illegitimate

Family situation at 7	Family situation at 11					
	Natural parents	Step-parents	Mother alone	Father alone	Other situations	Total
Natural parents	109 (91%)	0 (–)	8 (7%)	2 (2%)	1 (1%)	120 (100%)
Step-parents	1 (2%)	57 (92%)	3 (5%)	0 (–)	1 (2%)	62 (100%)
Mother alone	4 (9%)	4 (9%)	36 (82%)	0 (–)	0 (–)	44 (100%)
Father alone	0 (–)	0 (–)	0 (–)	0 (–)	0 (–)	0 (–)
Other situations	0 (–)	9 (17%)	8 (15%)	0 (–)	35 (67%)	52 (100%)
Not answered	8	2	3	0	3	16
Total	122	72	58	2	40	294

(b) Adopted

Family situation at 7	Family situation at 11		
	Adoptive parents	Other situations	Total
Adoptive parents	107 (96%)	5 (4%)	112 (100%)
Other situations	0 (–)	3 (100%)	3 (100%)
Total	107	8	115

(c) Legitimate

Family situation at 7	Family situation at 11						
	Natural parents	Step-parents	Adoptive parents	Mother alone	Father alone	Other situations	Total
Natural parents	10 628 (96%)	72 (1%)	1 (–)	238 (2%)	51 (0.5%)	60 (0.5%)	11 050 (100%)
Step-parents	1 (1%)	116 (89%)	0 (–)	6 (5%)	1 (1%)	7 (5%)	131 (100%)
Mother alone	7 (2%)	64 (22%)	0 (–)	214 (73%)	0 (–)	10 (3%)	295 (100%)
Father alone	0 (–)	3 (14%)	0 (–)	1 (4%)	17 (77%)	1 (4%)	22 (100%)
Other situations	12 (8%)	31 (20%)	1 (1%)	13 (8%)	11 (7%)	84 (55%)	152 (100%)
Not answered	358	19	1	31	4	8	421
Total	11 006	305	3	503	84	170	12 071

Natural parents at 7 years: Illeg/legit by natural parents at 11/other $\chi^2(1\mathrm{df}) = 10.3$**
Step parents at 7: Illeg/legit by step-parents at 11/other $\chi^2(1\mathrm{df}) = 0.2$
Mother alone at 7: Illeg/legit by mother alone at 11/other $\chi^2(1\mathrm{df}) = 1.3$
Illeg/legit: Change 7–11 $\chi^2(1\mathrm{df}) = 50.7$***

per cent of the illegitimate children who were living with their mothers alone at 7 were still living with them at 11, compared with 73 per cent of legitimate children living with mothers alone at 7, the difference was not statistically significant.

Family situation and social class

Social class will be considered in greater detail in Chapter 8. Here the relationship between social class at 11 and family situation is examined for the three legitimacy status groups (Table A7.2). It is clear that although illegitimate children were much less likely than legitimate children to be living with both their natural parents, there was no difference to this pattern depending on whether the illegitimate children came from non-manual or manual social class homes. Legitimate children who came from non-manual social class homes were, however, more likely still to be living with both their own parents at the age of 11 than those from manual homes. Where the children lived in a household with no male head, legitimate children were significantly more likely than illegitimate children to be living with their own mothers rather than in 'other situations', such as local authority care. There were no social class differences in the proportion of adopted children who were living in 'other situations' at the age of 11.

Children in care

Children are received into care for all sorts of reasons (Packman, 1968). Information from a special study of the children in the NCDS who had been in care by the age of 7 revealed that difficulty in finding accomodation was the most frequent reason for illegitimate children coming into care where their mothers were unsupported, while confinement or physical illness were more common reasons where their mothers were supported (Mapstone, 1969; Crellin et al., 1971). At present, comparable data are not available for the children who were first received into care between the ages of 7 and 11. Table 7.3 shows that 4 per cent of illegitimate children went into the care of a local authority or a voluntary society for the first time during these four years, compared with 1 per cent of legitimate children. However, although a relatively higher proportion of illegitimate children than legitimate children had been in care at some point up to the age of 11, it should be stressed that fewer than two out of ten of the illegitimate

TABLE 7.3 *Children in care*

Legitimacy status	Long stay care before 7	Short stay care before 7	In care between 7–11	Other answers	Never in care	Total	Not known
Illegitimate	15 (6%)	16 (6%)	10 (4%)	3 (1%)	225 (84%)	269 (100%)	25
Legitimate	64 (1%)	124 (1%)	122 (1%)	47 (–)	11155 (97%)	11512 (100%)	564

The figures for the adopted group have not been given, as a detailed check has revealed doubts about them (relating to some adoptive parents' uncertainty about the pre-adoption situation and agency practice). This will be investigated further during a new study of the children in care, currently being undertaken.

Illeg/legit by in care/never χ^2 (1df) = 143.6***

children had ever been in care. By far the greater volume of work for most child-care agencies, as far as numbers were concerned, would have come from legitimate children.

Turning to the family situation at 11, a higher proportion of illegitimate than legitimate children who were living with both their own parents had been in care at some time during their childhood (Table A7.3). One in four of the illegitimate children living with their mothers alone at 11 had been in care, compared with one in ten of the legitimate children. There was no significant difference in the proportions of illegitimate and legitimate children living with step-parents at 11 who had been in care, but the illegitimate children tended to come into care for the first time after the age of 7 rather than before it. In general, the findings up to the age of 11 continue to suggest that the reasons for admission to care may have varied between the illegitimate and legitimate children.

8
Background Characteristics

Social class

Social class is a convenient and useful indirect measure of many aspects of a child's environment, and an important predictor of ability and educational attainment as well as of other aspects of development. In studying the development of illegitimate and adopted children, and in making comparisons between these two groups and legitimate children, it is important to know whether or not their social class distributions are broadly similar or different.

The 7-year-old follow-up studies showed that, although there were no significant social class differences at birth between legitimate and illegitimate children, at 7 there were considerable class differences between the illegitimate, the adopted and the legitimate children (Crellin *et al.*, 1971). These differences were greatest between the illegitimate and the adopted groups of children where, for example, the proportion of adopted children living in middle-class homes at 7 was nearly five times as high as the proportion of illegitimate children living in such homes. It was expected that by the time these children reached 11 years there would be no substantial change in this pattern. After describing the comparative social class distributions at 11 of the three legitimacy status groups, we shall explore the relationship between 7-year-old and 11-year-old social class for these three groups, and then the stability and mobility of social class for the three groups of children since birth by comparing their social class of origin and their social class at 11.

Definitions

The National Child Development Study, in common with most other investigations, has taken the occupation of the male head of household as an indicator of social class. This is used by the Registrar General of England and Wales in Census reports, and by the Registrar General for Scotland in his annual returns of births and deaths. The classification used consists of the following six occupational groups:

Social class

I	Higher professional	⎫
II	Other professional and technical	⎬ Non-manual
III (non-manual)	Other non-manual occupations	('middle-class')
III (manual)	Skilled manual	⎫ Manual
IV	Semi-skilled manual	⎬ ('working-class')
V	Unskilled manual	⎭

With few exceptions, the first three groups contain white-collar jobs, and these will be termed either 'non-manual' or 'middle-class'. The occupations classified in the other groups are almost exclusively of a manual nature, and these will be referred to as 'manual' or 'working class'.

Most children in this study will, therefore, be assigned a social class position based on their mother's husband's occupation at the time of the survey. But a number of children in this study at the age of 7 and/or 11 were living in fatherless families and, therefore, there was no measure of their current social class position. Consequently these children were not assigned a social class position but have been described as having 'no male head' of household.

A further problem arises in relation to the illegitimate children. At the time of their birth information was not systematically collected in the Perinatal Mortality Survey concerning the natural father's occupation, as it was for legitimate children. Although information on their mother's occupation immediately preceding and during pregnancy was collected, it was not thought appropriate to use these data because of the youthfulness of many of the mothers of the illegitimate children, the fact that their jobs may not have been their usual ones, and also because of the difficulty of making comparisons with mothers of legitimate children (64 per cent of whom were not working at the start of their pregnancy). To overcome this difficulty it was decided to use the information collected on the mother's father's occupation at the time when the mother left school. Strictly speaking, this represents the social class of origin of the mother rather than that of the child, but it does have the advantage of providing more comprehensive data for comparing the three legitimacy status groups.

Thus the same procedure as that used in the 7-year studies has been continued, despite objections raised by Gill and his colleagues (Gill, 1977). In their studies of 'anomalous' family circumstances in Aberdeen they have used the mother's own occupation at the time of marriage or at first pregnancy (even though there could be several years in between these events). However, their data, in fact, show only very small differences according to whether the wife's, her husband's or her father's ocupation is used. It should also be noted that Gill and his colleagues did not use the Registrar General's classification of occupation.

One of Gill's criticisms of the National Child Development Study data relates to the proportion of mothers whose father's occupations could not be classified. A detailed study of the relevant table (available from the British Library) shows that of the 20 per cent of fathers whose jobs were not classified, 10 per cent were dead, 2 per cent were sick, unemployed or retired, and in only 8 per cent of cases was the father's social class not classified because it was not known. Although we think Gill's criticisms should be answered, it must be obvious that neither method is perfect. However, we feel that the more comprehensive data obtained by using mother's father's social class justifies our continuing to use it as a measure of social class of origin. In particular, it enables some important questions about the children's development to be studied in greater detail.

Social class at 11

As expected, the social class distribution of the three legitimacy status groups at 11 was similar to that found at 7 (Table 8.1). The proportion of adopted children living in non-manual homes at 11 was five times as high as the proportion of illegitimate children living in such homes and was also considerably higher than the proportion of legitimate children. Nearly a quarter of the illegitimate children were living in families with no male head of household, compared with 4

TABLE 8.1   *Social class at 11*

Legitimacy status	Non-manual (NM)	Social class Manual (M)	No male head (NMH)	Total	Not known
Illegitimate	33 (12%)	183 (64%)	69 (24%)	285 (100%)	9
Adopted	65 (60%)	44 (40%)	0 (–)	109 (100%)	6
Legitimate	4 006 (34%)	7 373 (62%)	536 (4%)	11 915 (100%)	161

Illeg/legit by NM/M/NMH χ^2 (4df) = 259.2***
Illeg/legit by NM/M χ^2 (4df) = 37.1***
Adop/legit by NM/M χ^2 (4df) = 27.1***

per cent of legitimate children and none of the adopted. Although the social class distribution of the three legitimacy status groups shows considerable differences, the proportion of illegitimate children in manual homes (64 per cent) is similar to that of the legitimate children (62 per cent).

Relationship between 7-year and 11-year social class

Although the social class distributions at 7 and 11 were similar, one would expect there to be a certain amount of movement between social class groups taking place for individual children, particularly in view of the changes in family situation in all three legitimacy status groups. Table 8.2 shows that there was in fact quite a complex pattern of changes in social class. Among children living in non-manual social class homes at 7, half of those who were illegitimate were living either in manual homes or in ones with no male head at 11, compared with approximately one in every seven of those who were legitimate. Among children living in manual homes, the proportions of illegitimate children (85 per cent) and legitimate children (87 per cent) who were still in the same social class homes at 11 were very similar, but illegitimate children were more likely than legitimate children to be living in households with no male head and less likely to have changed to non-manual homes at 11. Adopted children showed no significant differences in terms of social mobility from legitimate children. They were, however, much more likely to be upwardly mobile from manual to non-manual than illegitimate children, who were more likely to be downwardly mobile.

TABLE 8.2 *Relationship of social class at 11 to social class at 7 (children whose social class grouping is known at both ages)*

7-year social class	11-year social class			
	Non-manual	Manual	No male head	Total
(a) Non-manual				
Illegitimate	16 (50%)	12 (37%)	4 (13%)	32 (100%)
Adopted	52 (95%)	3 (5%)	0 (–)	55 (100%)
Legitimate	3 059 (86%)	408 (12%)	82 (2%)	3 549 (100%)
(b) Manual				
Illegitimate	11 (6%)	148 (85%)	15 (9%)	174 (100%)
Adopted	11 (22%)	40 (78%)	0 (–)	51 (100%)
Legitimate	768 (10%)	6 583 (87%)	182 (3%)	7 533 (100%)
(c) No male head				
Illegitimate	1 (2%)	7 (16%)	37 (82%)	45 (100%)
Adopted	1 (100%)	0 (–)	0 (–)	1 (100%)
Legitimate	21 (7%)	57 (19%)	220 (74%)	298 (100%)

NM at 7: Illeg/legit by 11-year social class (NM, M, NMH)	χ^2 (4df) = 36.8***
NM at 7: Adop/legit by 11-year social class (NM, M)	χ^2 (2df) = 1.5
NM at 7: Illeg/adop by 11-year social class (NM, M)	χ^2 (2df) = 17.5***
M at 7: Illeg/legit by 11-year social class (NM, M, NMH)	χ^2 (4df) = 28.2***
M at 7: Adop/legit by 11-year social class (NM, M)	χ^2 (2df) = 5.5
M at 7: Illeg/adop by 11-year social class (NM, M)	χ^2 (2df) = 8.8*
NMH at 7: Illeg/legit by 11-year social class (NM, M, NMH)	χ^2 (2df) = 2.0

Social class of origin compared with social class at 11

When the social class of the homes the children were living in at 11 was compared with their social class of origin (that is, based on the mother's father's social class), clear differences could be seen in the three legitimacy status groups (Table A8.1). In order to provide a more complete picture the results include those children whose social class of origin was either not classified or not known.

Adopted children who came from a non-manual social class of origin were likely also to be living in such homes at 11. Those who came from manual homes of origin were as likely to be in non-manual as manual homes at 11.

On the other hand, illegitimate children who came from a non-manual social class of origin were likely either to be in manual homes at 11 or with no male head of household. The majority of illegitimate children who came from a manual social class of origin were also living in such homes, but those who changed social class were more likely to be in homes with no male head than in non-manual homes. Legitimate children who changed from a manual social class of origin were, by contrast, more likely to be in non-manual homes at 11 than with no male head of household.

Thus, although the changes noted between 7 and 11 showed a considerable amount of social mobility during those four years, the pattern seems to be one which has been going on since birth. Once children have been offered and placed for adoption, their social class is likely to continue to be non-manual or to become so, whereas illegitimate children who are not adopted are more likely to experience downward social mobility from birth or to be living in households with no male head. Although a somewhat higher proportion of legitimate children move down from non-manual to manual than move up from manual to non-manual, the proportions who are in households with no male head of household at 11 are similar whether the children came from non-manual or manual homes of origin.

Sex distribution

Although at the time of birth there was a slightly higher proportion of girls among those illegitimately born (52 per cent) than among the legitimate (48 per cent), this difference was not statistically significant. At 7 it was noted that proportionally more illegitimate girls than boys had been kept by their mothers, and there were now significant differences in the sex distribution both between the illegitimate and adopted and between the illegitimate and legitimate children (Crellin *et al.*, 1971). However, there was no significant difference in the proportion of boys and girls between the adopted and the legitimate children in the cohort (Seglow *et al.*, 1972). Unless the distribution in the three legitimacy status groups had become

biased, owing to attrition, there would be no reason for it to change at
the age of 11. Table 8.3 shows marked differences in the proportions
of girls and boys at 11 similar to those noted at the age of 7. Of
illegitimate children, 58 per cent were girls, but only 43 per cent of
the adopted were girls.

TABLE 8.3 *Sex distribution at 11*

Legitimacy status	Boy	Girl	Total
Illegitimate	124 (42 %)	170 (58 %)	294 (100 %)
Adopted	65 (57 %)	50 (43 %)	115 (100 %)
Legitimate	6 188 (51 %)	5 883 (49 %)	12 071 (100 %)

It is, therefore, important in considering the children's development to take account of their sex, particularly when comparing the
adopted and the illegitimate children, as differences may be accounted for by this factor rather than by their legitimacy status. This is
especially relevant for social adjustment in school, as boys in the
cohort as a whole were known to be less well adjusted than girls
(Davie *et al.*, 1972). The sex ratio may also be important, as noted in
Chapter 5, in relation to adoptive parents' preferences and attitudes.

It is possible that as there were fewer girls available, middle-class
adoptive parents might have been more successful in adopting them
than working-class adoptive parents. At the age of 11, however, there
was no significant difference in the social class distribution of the
adopted boys and girls (Table A8.2). It will be noted that there were
also no differences in the sex distribution for illegitimate or legitimate
children when social class was allowed for. Although the mother's
original decision whether to keep her illegitimate child or not may, in
some cases, have been influenced by the child's sex, this had not led to
girls being more likely to be in families with no male head than in
working-class or middle-class families by the age of 11.

When family situation was taken into account, there was a
tendency for a higher proportion of illegitimate than legitimate
children living with both natural parents to be girls (Table A8.3).
Although the proportion of illegitimate girls living with step-parents
at 11 was also higher than that for legitimate children, the difference
was not significant. Ferri (1976) has noted the tendency for children
in one-parent families (whatever their legitimacy status) to be cared
for by the parent of the same sex.

Family size

The interrelationship between family size and other home background factors, such as social class, crowding and amenities, and its
association with developmental outcomes has been shown by
Fogelman (1975) and others. Clearly family size is important in a
study of changing patterns of family composition, particularly where
the families in one of the groups (the adopted) were initially changed
by means of the adoption process. Subsequently there are likely to
have been changes in family size in all three legitimacy status groups
as a result of breaks in the family and changes of partners, and also as
a result of the addition of new births (or adoptions) and the departure
of older children from the household or their reaching the age of 21.
At 11 the same definition of family size was employed as at 7, that is,
the number of children under the age of 21 living in a household,
whatever their relationship to each other.

Family size at 11

The family size distribution at 11 (Table 8.4) is very similar to that
found at 7. At 11, illegitimate and adopted children were more likely
than legitimate children to be the only child in the household, as they
had been at 7, but the proportion of legitimate 'only' children was
slightly higher at 11 than it had been at 7, and that for the illegitimate
slightly lower. The proportion of illegitimate children in families of
five or more had increased since 7, whereas the proportion of
legitimate children in 'large' families was the same at both ages.

Family size and social class

Table A8.4 shows that when family size is looked at within social
class, there were significant differences between the three legitimacy
status groups. Adopted children from both non-manual and manual
homes tended to live in smaller families than either illegitimate or
legitimate children. This tendency was so marked that within the
adopted group there was no social class difference in family size
composition.

There were only a few illegitimate children in non-manual homes,
but there was a considerable difference in the size of their families
compared with legitimate children from similar homes, particularly

TABLE 8.4 *Family size at 11*

Legitimacy status	Family size at eleven					Total	NA
	1	2	3	4	5+		
Illegitimate	53 (19%)	69 (24%)	57 (20%)	45 (16%)	61 (21%)	285 (100%)	9
Adopted	35 (31%)	54 (48%)	13 (12%)	8 (7%)	2 (2%)	112 (100%)	3
Legitimate	1 281 (11%)	4 024 (33%)	3 058 (25%)	1 841 (15%)	1 820 (15%)	12 024 (100%)	52

Illeg/legit by family size (1; 2; 3; 4; 5+)
χ^2 (trend) $= 2.6$ (2df)
χ^2 (departure from trend) $= 23.7^{***}$ (6df)

Illeg/adop by family size (1; 2; 3; 4; 5+)
χ^2 (trend) $= 86.6^{***}$ (2df)
χ^2 (departure from trend) $= 6.8$ (6df)

Adop/legit by family size (1; 2; 3; 4; 5+)
χ^2 (trend) $= 49.2^{***}$ (2df)
χ^2 (departure from trend) $= 17.4^{**}$ (6df)

TABLE 8.5   Family size and family situation at 11

Family situation at 11	1	2	1-2 (small)	3-4 (medium)	5+ (large)	Total	NA
Natural parents – Illegit	9	24	33 (27%)	52 (43%)	37 (30%)	122 (100%)	0
– Legit	1 122	3 728	4 850 (44%)	4 507 (41%)	1 633 (15%)	10 990 (100%)	16
Step-parents – Illegit	6	21	27 (37%)	33 (46%)	12 (17%)	72 (100%)	0
– Legit	18	70	88 (29%)	145 (48%)	70 (23%)	303 (100%)	2
Mother alone – Illegit	20	12	32 (63%)	11 (21%)	8 (16%)	51 (100%)	7
– Legit	74	155	229 (45%)	187 (38%)	79 (16%)	495 (100%)	8
Father alone – Illegit	1	1	2 (100%)	0 (–)	0 (–)	2 (100%)	0
– Legit	19	34	53 (64%)	22 (26%)	8 (10%)	83 (100%)	1
Other situations – Illegit	17	11	28 (74%)	6 (16%)	4 (10%)	38 (100%)	2
– Legit	47	36	83 (55%)	38 (25%)	30 (20%)	151 (100%)	19
Adoptive parents	31	53	84 (79%)	20 (19%)	2 (2%)	106 (100%)	1

Natural parents: Illeg/legit by family size (1 – 2/3 – 4/5 +)
χ^2 (trend)   = 17.7***(1df)
χ^2 (departure from trend)   = 1.5   (1df)

Step-parents: Illeg/legit by family size (1 – 2/3 – 4/5 +)
χ^2 (trend)   = 2.5   (1df)
χ^2 (departure from trend)   = 0.0   (1df)

Mother alone:Illeg/legit by family size (1 – 2/3 – 4/5 +)
χ^2 (trend)   = 2.3   (1df)
χ^2 (departure from trend)   = 4.4* (1df)

in the higher proportion living in large families. By contrast, there was no significant difference in family composition between illegitimate and legitimate children from manual homes. Some of these differences and similarities are probably associated with family situation as much as with social class.

Family size and family situation

When the number of children living in the various family situations at 11 was examined, illegitimate children living with both natural parents were less likely to be in 'small' families and more likely to be in 'large' families than legitimate children (Table 8.5). There was no significant difference in the size of family of illegitimate or legitimate children living with step-parents. Illegitimate children living with their mothers alone were, however, somewhat more likely than legitimate children to be in small families and, in fact, to be 'only' children, but the proportions in large families were similar. It is interesting to note that a high proportion of the illegitimate children living in 'other situations' (many of them substitute families) were in small families. In this respect they appear to be similar to adopted children, 79 per cent of whom were in small families. In both these groups and for the illegitimate children living with their mothers alone the tendency to small family size may be involuntary to a greater degree than for legitimate children. In the case of the adopted children this can be related to difficulties in adopting even one or two children. In those cases where the mother kept her child but never married, or where the child has had to live with other caretakers, the chances of there being other children in the household appear to be reduced.

9

Families on Low Incomes

Although the measurement of poverty in Britain is imprecise, large numbers of families and their children are living on low incomes. One 'official' definition of poverty is represented by the Supplementary Benefits Commission's scale rates, which are laid down by Parliament, and these provide a national minimum standard of living below which the Government feels no household should fall. It has been argued that the official measures of poverty are inadequate, based as they are on some notion of subsistence rather than on the average living standards of the wider community. However, even those critical of the subsistence notion acknowledge that it has at least the advantage of being the operational definition of the minimum standard of living at any particular time (Abel-Smith and Townsend, 1965). The head of a family is eligible to draw supplementary benefit where he or she is not in full-time work or is not required to register for work and his or her income falls short of the prescribed level.

Children in families in receipt of supplementary benefit are automatically entitled to free school meals. Other families are also entitled to claim free school meals even though the head of household may be working, or receiving sickness or unemployment benefit paid on scales which may work out at a higher rate than supplementary benefit. The criteria for eligibility change from time to time, but the basic principle lies in fixing an income limit which allows for the deduction of various expenses such as rent and takes into account factors such as family size.

It is common knowledge, however, that not all children who are entitled to free school meals have them. The Circumstances of Families Report (MSS, 1967) found that only 50 per cent of children of families with an income at or below national assistance level were receiving free school meals. This led to the Government launching an intensive effort to improve take-up at the end of 1967. By 1969 it was estimated that about 80 per cent of those eligible were claiming. This figure was challenged by the CPAG (Lister, 1974), who claimed that it was an underestimate, but even if it was correct, there were still many children, one in five, who could have been eating free school meals who were not doing so. Even despite the widespread publicity, ignorance of entitlement may have been the explanation in some cases, but a number of studies have indicated that the main reason is the stigma associated with claiming benefits. For some this feeling is derived from humiliating or discriminatory experiences. The methods used to collect dinner money, and the identification of 'free dinner children' by coloured or marked tickets, separate queues or separate tables, or even by casual remarks from staff or pupils, have repeatedly been criticised (see Lynes, 1969).

During the course of the parental interview, carried out when the NCDS children were 11, details were obtained of the source of income of each child's family during the preceding 12 months. Information was also obtained as to whether any child of the family was receiving free school meals at the time of the interview, which meant that the family was living on a low income. These two measures provide some estimate of the extent to which children in the three legitimacy status groups were living in families whose material welfare had been partly or totally dependent upon state support at the time of the 1969 follow-up or in the year before. They are, however, likely to give an underestimate of the full extent of poverty, as there will have been children living in families who were eligible for free school meals but who, for the reasons suggested above, were not having them; moreover, some parents may have omitted to mention receipt of supplementary benefit as a source of income in the previous 12 months, or could have been eligible but decided not to claim. It should also be noted that in some families the person receiving supplementary benefit might be, for example, an elderly relative, and the family, as such, would not become entitled to free school meals.

Although the analysis which follows divides the children in families receiving supplementary benefit and free school meals into (a) those receiving both, (b) those who have received supplementary benefit only and (c) those only in receipt of free school meals, the divisions should not, for the reasons given above, be taken too rigidly.

Receipt of supplementary benefit or free school meals at 11

A third of the illegitimate children were living in families who reported that they were in receipt of either or both supplementary benefit and free school meals, compared with 4 per cent of adopted children and 13 per cent of the legitimate. Four times as many illegitimate as legitimate children were receiving both benefits, and altogether at least 27 per cent of the illegitimate children were in families living on low incomes at the actual time of the study, as they reported receipt of free school meals. This demonstrates the very unfavourable financial circumstances of these children compared with legitimate children, 10 per cent of whom were living in families receiving free school meals (see Table 9.1).

It seems probable that if the families of the illegitimate children had been living in financial hardship for longer periods than the families of legitimate children, they may have been more likely to claim benefits than families in short-term need. Information on the uptake of benefits was not obtained at the 7-year-old follow-up. However, evidence from the subsequent 16-year-old follow-up does show that children in families receiving supplementary benefit both in 1969 and in 1974 were at a greater material disadvantage than those receiving supplementary benefit at only one age (Essen and Ghodsian, 1977).

Receipt of supplementary benefit or free school meals and family situation

The likelihood of being dependent upon state support is related to family situation. This was certainly so among the illegitimate and legitimate children in our study. (All the four adopted children whose families were in receipt of benefits were still living with both their adoptive parents.)

Children living with their mother alone were much more likely than any of the other children to be living in families in receipt of supplementary benefit and free school meals, and there were no significant differences between legitimate and illegitimate children in this respect (see Table 9.2). No less than 60 per cent of the illegitimate and 66 per cent of the legitimate in fatherless families were receiving at least one of the benefits and in almost all cases the families were, in fact, in receipt of free school meals at the time of the study. Neither of the two illegitimate children living in motherless families

TABLE 9.1 *Receipt of supplementary benefit (SB) and free school means (FSM) at 11*

Legitimacy status	SB and FSM	FSM only	SB only	Neither benefit	Total	NA
Illegitimate	47 (17%)	29 (10%)	17 (6%)	190 (67%)	283 (100%)	11
Adopted	2 (2%)	2 (2%)	0 (—)	108 (96%)	112 (100%)	3
Legitimate	521 (4%)	661 (6%)	348 (3%)	10 347 (87%)	11 877 (100%)	199

Illeg/legit by SB + FSM/others χ^2 (2df) = 90.0***
Illeg/legit by FSM/no FSM χ^2 (2df) = 83.3***
Adop/legit by SB or FSM/neither χ^2 (2df) = 7.8*

TABLE 9.2   *Receipt of supplementary benefit (SB) and free school meals (FSM) related to family situation at 11*

Family situation		In receipt of:					
		SB + FSM	FSM only	SB only	Neither	Total	NA
Natural parents	Illegitimate	11 (9%)	15 (13%)	9 (7%)	84 (71%)	119 (100%)	3
	Legitimate	281 (2%)	510 (5%)	295 (3%)	9754 (90%)	10840 (100%)	164
Step-parents	Illegitimate	5 (7%)	6 (8%)	4 (6%)	57 (79%)	72 (100%)	0
	Legitimate	20 (7%)	29 (10%)	12 (4%)	239 (79%)	300 (100%)	6
Mother alone	Illegitimate	26 (50%)	4 (8%)	1 (2%)	21 (40%)	52 (100%)	6
	Legitimate	194 (39%)	105 (21%)	26 (5%)	169 (34%)	494 (100%)	10
Father alone	Illegitimate	0 (–)	0 (–)	0 (–)	2 (100%)	2 (100%)	0
	Legitimate	9 (11%)	7 (8%)	4 (5%)	64 (76%)	84 (100%)	0
Other situations	Illegitimate	5 (13%)	4 (11%)	3 (8%)	26 (68%)	38 (100%)	2
	Legitimate	16 (11%)	10 (7%)	1 (1%)	117 (81%)	144 (100%)	24
Adoptive parents		2 (2%)	2 (2%)	0 (–)	102 (96%)	106 (100%)	2

Natural parents: Illeg./legit. by SB or FSM/neither χ^2(1df) = 46.1***
Step parents: Illeg./legit. by SB or FSM/neither χ^2(1df) = 0.0
Mother alone: Illeg./legit. by SB or FSM/neither χ^2(1df) = 0.5

were receiving benefits, but almost a fifth of legitimate children living with lone fathers were in families receiving free school meals.

Illegitimate children living with their natural parents were three times more likely than legitimate children living with their own parents to be in receipt of benefits; the proportions receiving supplementary benefit, free school meals or both benefits all show the same relative difference between illegitimate and legitimate children. One reason for this probably lies in the fact that there was a higher proportion of illegitimate children living with both natural parents in large sized families (see Table 8.5).

The proportion of illegitimate and legitimate children living in step-families who were receiving benefits was very similar, with 7 per cent in each group in receipt of both supplementary benefit and free school meals. Among illegitimate children those living with step-parents had the smallest proportion of any of the family situations in receipt of benefits (although the difference in this respect between illegitimate children in step-families and those living with both natural parents was not significant). The difference between children in step-families and those with both their own parents was more noticeable among the legitimate, where 90 per cent of those living with their natural parents were reported to be receiving neither benefit, compared with 79 per cent in step-families. Once again, differences in family size may partially explain the situation (see Table 8.5).

The fact that one in three of 11-year-old illegitimate children, whatever their family situation, were living on poverty incomes, as represented by the measures used in this study, can only be a cause for concern. This is particularly so, as the proportion at 11 is likely to be an underestimate and an unknown, but certainly higher, proportion will have been brought up on low incomes at some stage of their lives. The vulnerability of one-parent families in this respect reiterates the findings of the special studies on these families (Ferri 1976; Ferri and Robinson, 1976). In contrast, nearly all the adopted children enjoyed much better material circumstances, a finding which accords with the high proportion living in middle-class homes.

10

Housing Conditions

Crowding

The amount of overcrowding within a home provides a direct measure of the housing conditions in which children are growing up, compared with more generalised assumptions about certain forms of tenure. Previous work from the NCDS has drawn attention to the prevalence of overcrowding in the study children's homes and to factors associated with this situation (Davie *et al.*, 1972; Wedge and Prosser, 1973; Essen and Parrinder, 1975). Overcrowding was found to be more common among children than among the general population, but the extent of overcrowding varied according to type of tenure, with the prevalence highest in the furnished rented sector but also surprisingly high in council housing. There were clear associations with social class, and not unexpectedly, with family size. As the children grew older, overcrowding reduced somewhat, and nearly twice as many children had ceased to be overcrowded by 11 as had become so between 7 and 11 (Essen and Parrinder, 1975).

In the present study the measure of overcrowding used is the same as in previous NCDS studies and the 1961 census, which, as has been pointed out, is not a generous one. A household is defined as overcrowded if it has more than 1.5 persons per room (which includes a kitchen only if used as a living room).

Crowding at 11

Table 10.1 shows that illegitimate children were more likely to be living in overcrowded housing at 11 than legitimate children, while adopted children were considerably less likely than those in the other

TABLE 10.1 *Crowding at 11†*

Legitimacy status	Persons per room				Total	NK
	≤ 1.0	> 1.0	> 1.5	> 2.0		
Illegitimate	140 (49%)	98 (34%)	41 (14%)	7 (2%)	286 (100%)	8
Adopted	101 (90%)	8 (7%)	3 (3%)	– (–)	112 (100%)	3
Legitimate	7 343 (61%)	3 289 (27%)	1 104 (9%)	290 (2%)	12 026 (100%)	50

† Children are defined as crowded where the occupancy is more than one and a half persons to a room.

Illeg/legit by crowding at 11 ($\leq 1.0, -1.5, -2.0, > 2.0$)
χ^2 (trend) = 11.8 (2df)**
χ^2 (departure from trend) = 4.7 (4df)

Adop/legit by crowding at 11 ($\leq 1.0, > 1.5$) χ^2 2(df) = 38.4*** two legitimacy status groups to be in this situation. None of the adopted children came into the most severely overcrowded group (>2.0 persons per room) and it is likely that the smaller size of adoptive families (see Chapter 8) also partly accounted for the very high proportion (90 per cent) who were in the most spacious accommodation (≤ 1.0 person per room). As well as there being a higher proportion of illegitimate children in homes which were, by definition, overcrowded there was also a lower proportion (49 per cent) in the most spaciously housed group (≤ 1.0 person per room), compared with legitimate children (61 per cent).

Crowding at 7 and 11

Turning to the situation at the ages of 7 and 11, we found that more than one in every four of the illegitimate children were living in overcrowded conditions at one or both of these ages (Table A10.1). This is likely to be an underestimate of the full extent of overcrowding, as data are only available at each follow-up and not between the two follow-ups, or before the age of 7. However, although the extent of overcrowding which illegitimate children experienced at either 7 or 11 was significantly greater than that experienced by legitimate children (27 per cent as against 17 per cent), there was no significant difference in the proportions of legitimate and illegitimate children who were overcrowded at *both* the ages of 7 and 11.

Crowding and family situation at 11

Table A10.2 shows up immediately one of the inherent limitations of the definition of overcrowding for this particular study, namely, that living in a one-parent family appears to reduce the level of overcrowding whatever the realities of the situation. The general problem has been discussed in some detail by Ferri (1976). Here it is sufficient to note that although a slightly higher proportion of illegitimate children living with a lone mother were in overcrowded homes at 11, compared with legitimate children with lone mothers, the difference was not significant. (A number of the family situations contained within the 'other situations' category would be subject to the same problem with the definition of overcrowding, and this may account for the somewhat smaller proportions who were overcrowded.)

Illegitimate children living with their own parents were the most likely to be in overcrowded homes (25 per cent), and a further 36 per cent were living in homes which could be considered fairly cramped. Illegitimate children living with step-parents were somewhat, but not significantly, less likely than those with both natural parents to be overcrowded. Among legitimate children the pattern was different, as a significantly higher proportion of children in step-families (16 per cent) than children with their own parents (11 per cent) were living in overcrowded homes. The percentage of legitimate children living with step-parents who were in overcrowded homes was actually slightly, but not significantly, higher than that of illegitimate children with step-parents.

Amenities

The availability of amenities within a home provides another measure of housing conditions. Data were collected for the NCDS relating to access to an indoor lavatory, a hot-water supply and a bathroom. These have been combined into an 'amenity scale', which shows whether a household has sole use of all three, sole use of two, sole use of one, or shared or no use of all three.

In some households it may not be a great inconvenience to share perhaps a bathroom or a lavatory (or to have only an outside and not an indoor lavatory), but if the family has to share all these basic facilities or has no access to them at all, then daily life is beset with problems. These problems are frequently linked with other housing problems (such as overcrowding) and with such difficulties as low status and low pay, all of which add to a disadvantaged environment in which to bring up children (Wedge and Prosser, 1973). In the cohort as a whole 12 per cent of children were found to be sharing or lacking at least one of the amenities at 11 (Essen and Parrinder, 1975). Children living in privately rented homes were the most likely to share or lack amenities, and this has also been found to be so for the general population (Milner Holland Report, Ministry of Housing, 1965; OPCS, 1973). There was evidence of some improvement in the availability of amenities between the two NCDS follow-ups in 1965 and 1969, although this was not so apparent for those living in council rented accommodation (Essen and Parrinder, 1975).

Amenities at 11

The majority of children, irrespective of their legitimacy status, had the sole use of all amenities (Table 10.2). However, illegitimate children were more likely than the other children to be living in homes deficient in one or more of the standard amenities, as 26 per cent shared or lacked at least one of them, compared with 3 per cent of adopted children and 12 per cent of the legitimate. None of the adopted children shared or lacked all three amenities, compared with 10 per cent of illegitimate children. The proportion of illegitimate children in this situation was three times as high as that for legitimate children (3 per cent).

Amenities at 7 and 11

When access to amenities at the ages of 7 and 11 was compared, the privileged position of the adopted children stood out very clearly, as 94 per cent were living at both ages in homes with all amenities and only 1 per cent shared or lacked all amenities at both ages (Table A10.3). By contrast only 57 per cent of illegitimate children had lived at both ages in homes with all amenities, and 7 per cent shared or lacked all amenities at 7 and 11. Legitimate children came between the other two legitimacy status groups, as their homes were not as well provided for as those of adopted children; but they were considerably better equipped than the homes of illegitimate children in that 80 per cent had sole use of all three amenities and only 2 per cent shared or had no use of all three at 7 and 11.

Amenities and family situation at 11

When access to amenities is looked at for each family situation, it can be seen that a similar proportion of illegitimate children living with both their own parents and with their mothers alone were sharing or lacking all three amenities (Table A10.4). Illegitimate children from these two family situations were more likely than legitimate children living with both parents or with a lone mother to be sharing or lacking one or more amenity. Children living with step-parents, however, showed no significant difference in their access to amenities according to their legitimacy status.

TABLE 10.2 *Amenities at 11*

Legitimacy status	Sole use all 3	Sole use 2	Sole use 1	Shared/no use all 3	Total	NA
Illegitimate	210 (74%)	25 (9%)	20 (7%)	28 (10%)	283 (100%)	11
Adopted	109 (97%)	3 (3%)	– (–)	– (–)	112 (100%)	3
Legitimate	10 521 (88%)	729 (6%)	332 (3%)	311 (3%)	11 893 (100%)	183

Illeg/legit by amenities at 11 (sole use all, sole 2, sole 1, shared all)

χ^2 (trend) $= 29.2(2df)***$

χ^2 (departure from trend) $= 0.8(4df)$

Adop/legit by sole use all 3/others $\chi^2(2df) = 7.7*$

Tenure

Tenure provides an indicator of the availability of housing in the various sectors and the ability of families to acquire access to that section of the market. There is known to be a relationship between tenure and social class and also financial situation (Davie *et al.*, 1972). However, housing conditions can vary enormously within the same sector (Donnison, 1967; Cullingworth Report, Ministry of Housing, 1969; Greve *et al.*, 1971). Partly for this reason and partly because crowding and access to amenities provided better measures of housing conditions, it was decided to omit tenure from the later developmental analyses (Chapters 12–14). The data are, nevertheless, of considerable interest, and have, therefore, been summarised here. The types of tenure considered were the following: owner-occupied (or in process of being bought); rented from a local authority; privately rented, either furnished or unfurnished; and accommodation tied to occupation or for some reason rent-free.

The pattern of tenure at 11

Table 10.3 clearly demonstrates that there are marked differences in the type of tenure in which the study children were living at 11, depending on their legitimacy status. Illegitimate children were less likely to be living in owner-occupied homes than adopted children and legitimate children. One reason for there being such a high proportion of adopted children living in this type of tenure at 11 was likely to be associated with their middle-class social background (see Table 8.1). Housing is also a factor which has usually been taken into consideration by adoption agencies and, where middle-class standards have operated, the type of tenure, in particular, may have been used as an indicator for assessment. The 1971 General Household Survey (OPCS, 1973) found that 49 per cent of homes in Great Britain were owned. As the Survey refers to households and the present study to children, the figures are not directly comparable, but the proportion of legitimate children living in the owner-occupied sector (46 per cent) corresponds more closely than those in the other two legitimacy status groups to the percentage in the population as a whole.

Over half the illegitimate children were living in council accom-

TABLE 10.3 *Tenure at 11*

Legitimacy status	Tenure at eleven				
	Owned	Council rented	Privately rented	Tied to occupation	Total	Other/NA
Illegitimate	75 (26%)	159 (56%)	40 (14%)	11 (4%)	285 (100%)	9
Adopted	73 (65%)	29 (26%)	5 (4%)	5 (4%)	112 (100%)	3
Legitimate	5 521 (46%)	5 117 (43%)	842 (7%)	525 (4%)	12 005 (100%)	71

Illeg/legit by tenure (own; counc. rent; priv. rent; tied) χ^2(6df) = 54.2***
Adop/legit by tenure (own; counc. rent; priv. rent; tied) χ^2(6df) = 17.2**
Illeg/adop by tenure (own; counc. rent; priv. rent; tied) χ^2(6df) = 54.3***

modation in 1969, compared with a quarter of the adopted children and two-fifths of the legitimate. For both illegitimate and legitimate children, but particularly the illegitimate, this proportion is higher than for the proportion of households found to be living in such accommodation by the General Household Survey (31 per cent). Council accommodation was likely to have all the basic amenities, but some families were likely to be overcrowded (Essen and Parrinder, 1975).

Only a minority of the study children were living in the privately rented sector of housing at the age of 11, but the likelihood of this was greater for illegitimate children than for adopted or legitimately born children. The numbers of children who were living in rent-free or tied accommodation were small, and showed no differences in proportions for the three legitimacy status groups. The proportions are similar to that found in the 1971 General Household Survey (5 per cent), although the survey includes other miscellaneous types of housing in this category. Most tenants of rented or tied accommodation had no security of tenure in 1969, nor did they have the right to appeal to a rent tribunal.

Tenure and family situation at 11

Some illegitimate children had a better chance than others of being in owner-occupied homes. For example, 32 per cent of those living with natural parents were growing up in such homes at the age of 11, compared with 12 per cent of those living with their mothers alone (Table A10.5). These figures were, however, significantly lower than the proportions in owner-occupied homes of legitimate children living with both natural parents (47 per cent) or with their mother alone (27 per cent). Although a lower proportion of illegitimate than legitimate children living with step-parents were in owner-occupied homes, this difference did not reach statistical significance.

There was a higher proportion of illegitimate than legitimate children from each family situation in council housing at 11. Nearly twice the proportion of illegitimate than legitimate children living with both natural parents were in privately rented accommodation, but the proportions in privately rented accommodation of legitimate and illegitimate children living with step-parents were very alike.

A comparison of tenure at the ages of 7 and 11

The decline in the privately rented sector and increases in the owner-occupied and local authority sectors should be reflected in changes in the type of tenure of the homes in which the children were living in 1969 compared with 1965. It is probable, though, that the data presented here give an underestimate of the amount of change, as the families of children for whom data at both ages were not available may have been more likely to have changed their tenure during this period of time.

On the whole, children who were living in owner-occupied homes at 7 were also likely to be doing so at 11 (Table A10.6). Nevertheless, the three legitimacy status groups were not equally stable, and illegitimate children were the least likely to be living in this type of accommodation at both ages. It is interesting to note that the majority of the illegitimate children who changed from owner-occupied homes by 1969 were living in council-rented homes, whereas only just over half the legitimate children who changed went to this form of tenure.

The picture regarding council-rented accommodation showed no significant differences between the legitimacy status groups. Among those who were living in council-rented homes at 7, 87 per cent of the adopted children, 91 per cent of the legitimate and 94 per cent of the illegitimate were also living in this sector at 11.

As expected, at least half the children in each legitimacy status group who were living in private rented accommodation at 7 were not doing so four years later. Although little difference was found in the proportions of illegitimate and legitimate children remaining in private rented homes at 11, a significantly higher proportion of legitimate than illegitimate children changed to owner-occupied homes by 11, while illegitimate children more often moved to council-rented homes.

In all, 20 per cent of the illegitimate children experienced a change in the type of tenure in which they were living between the ages of 7 and 11, compared with 8 per cent of adopted children and 14 per cent of the legitimate. It will come as little surprise that among both the illegitimate and the legitimate children a higher proportion of those living with step-parents at 11 than of those in the various other family situations had experienced a change of tenure since the age of 7 (Table

S10.1). More of the legitimate children living in one-parent families and in 'other situations' who changed tenure moved to council housing than to other sectors. Thus, in tenure, as in other respects, there appeared to be considerable similarities between legitimate children no longer living with both their own parents and illegitimate children as a group.

Part III

The Children at 11: their Development and Progress since 7

11

General Note on the Analyses of Variance

In the chapters which follow we shall be looking at three areas of children's development at 11: firstly, their physical development, as measured by their height; secondly, their educational attainment, as measured by their scores in tests of reading and maths; and thirdly, their adjustment to school as measured by the Bristol Social Adjustment Guide. These measures will be described more fully in the relevant chapters.

After looking at the overall results in each of these developmental areas for children who were illegitimate or adopted or legitimate, we shall consider the relationship of these results with other home and family characteristics. These factors (detailed below) are first looked at either singly, or together with one or two factors only, in relation to each developmental outcome. Then all the factors are included in a joint analysis which shows their adjusted relationship with, for example, height, after allowing for the relationship of the factors to each other and to height. This means that, in the case of height, we can first see whether adopted children on average are taller than other children. Then we can see whether, for instance, adopted children are still on average taller than other children of the same sex and social class, or with access to the same number of amenities. Finally, we look to see whether adopted children are still likely to be taller than other children who share the same characteristics on all the factors included in the analysis (for example, middle-class boys from small families, not receiving free school meals, not living in over-crowded homes and having access to all basic amenities).

The term 'interaction' will be encountered at times in the text. After examining the straightforward differences among the groups of children, and then the effect on these of allowing for other background variables, tests are carried out for interactions, that is, for whether the differences found between, say, the adopted and the illegitimate are constant across the different categories of the other variables. If no significant interactions are found, then such differences can be assumed to be constant, for example, for each social class, for each family size, and for both sexes. Where a significant interaction does emerge, this is described and discussed in the text.

After looking at the broad differences between adopted, illegitimate and legitimate children, we ask whether the family situations may account for such differences or else vary the results. As the children were living in a wide variety of family situations (see Chapter 7), it is necessary to limit the groups to provide reasonable numbers for analysis; the groups are detailed below. We also wanted to include a measure of the extent of stability in the family situation, as we were already trying to determine whether the legitimacy status of the children at birth was associated with differences in their development at 11. If we had children in some groups who had remained in very stable parental-care situations while others had been changing a lot, it would be very difficult to tell whether differences between the groups were due to changes taking place in the family situation rather than to the children's legitimacy status. We therefore selected children who were reported to be living in the same family situations at both the ages of 7 and 11. Although this is a relatively crude measure of stability, and there may have been changes of parents between the ages of 7 and 11 of which we are unaware, evidence from studies of family breakdown (Herzog and Sudia, 1968; Rutter, 1972; Ferri, 1976) suggests that continuity of parenting is an important element in children's development. For this reason also we wished to include some groups of children who had experienced changes of parent figures by the age of 7, to see whether they differed from children living with both their own parents or with two adoptive parents. This would indicate whether and to what extent it was the change of parent or of difference in legitimacy status which might account for some children doing better than others. We were not able to include children living with their mothers alone in this analysis, as we could not assign them to a social class group and continue to identify, separately, the effect of their being with lone mothers.

A further question arose, concerning the progress between the ages of 7 and 11 of children in the different legitimacy status groups. Adopted children had, for instance, been found to be doing better than illegitimate children in reading at the age of 7 (Seglow *et al.,* 1972). If they were still doing better at 11, had they actually improved in their performance relative to that of the illegitimate children, so that the gap had widened? Or had the gap narrowed since the age of 7, although the illegitimate children had not 'caught up' with adopted children? In order to look at this question we carried out a joint analysis for the three legitimacy status groups, including their test scores at 7. In this way each child's score at 11 was measured in terms of a given score at 7 (for further details see Appendix 1). Such an analysis was not carried out for height because of the complications of differing rates of change according to age and the onset of puberty.

The legitimacy status groups

Illegitimate children
Adopted children
Legitimate children

Potentially, all the children in these three groups at 11 (see Table 6.1) were eligible for inclusion in these analyses. However, they needed to have data on *all* the factors included in the analyses as well as test scores, or BSAG rating or height measurement. As can be seen from the tables in Part II, for most of the variables there were a few children with missing data, and these children have had to be excluded from the analyses. A comparison of the differences in scores between the legitimacy status groups for all the children with developmental scores and for the children included in the joint analysis showed that the latter were representative of all the children in their group.

The family situation groups

(a) Legitimate children living with both natural parents at 7 and 11.
(b) Legitimate children living with one natural parent and one step-parent at 7 and 11.
(c) Illegitimately born children living with two adoptive parents at 7 and 11.
(d) Illegitimate children living with both natural parents at 7 and 11.
(e) Illegitimate children living with one natural parent and one step-parent at 7 and 11.

Group (c) is virtually the same as that described as 'the adopted children' elsewhere in the study, except for the exclusion of eight children who were living in 'other situations' at 11.

A full description of the definitions of the parental care situations can be found in Chapter 7. Further descriptive tables relating to the groups selected for analysis can be found in the supplementary tables (available, on request, from the British Library – see Appendix 3).

The other factors (independent variables) in the analyses

Sex: boy, girl

Social class:	non-manual at origin	non-manual at 11
	manual at origin	manual at 11
	non-manual at origin	manual at 11
	manual at origin	non-manual at 11
	non-manual at origin	no male head at 11
	manual at origin	no male head at 11

(The final two are not for the analysis of family situation)

Family size (that is, number of children in household under 21): 1–2, 3–4, 5+

Receiving free school meals: yes, no

Crowding: ≤ 1.5, > 1.5 persons per room

Household amenities (indoor lavatory, bathroom and hot-water supply combined as follows): sole use of all three; sole use of two; sole use of one; shared or no use of all three

Mother's height: (only for analysis of height; mother, in this case, is the child's natural mother)

Further details of the social class definitions can be found in Chapter 8. In the analyses of variance we have used a composite measure of social class which enables social class of origin and social class at 11 to be considered jointly or separately. This relates the birth situation to the current one, and is of particular interest with respect to the adopted children, all of whom have changed parental care figures since birth. It is also of great interest with respect to the illegitimate children, as it relates to questions about the extent to which their development depends on subsequent events rather than, or as much as, the situation into which they were born.

12

Height

The height of a child has been suggested to be a 'very useful indicator of general physical, development and its study may give valuable pointers to circumstances before, during or after birth which have an adverse effect upon development' (Davie *et al.*, 1972). The relationship between children's height and factors such as social class, family size and their own mother's height has been demonstrated in a number of other studies (see Douglas and Simpson, 1964; Grant, 1964; Tanner, Goldstein and Whitehouse, 1970).

At the time of the 7-year-old study the children's teachers reported that the adopted children were taller than either illegitimate or legitimate children, but that the illegitimate children did not differ in height from those who were legitimate (Crellin *et al.*, 1971; Seglow *et al.*, 1972). Although various other medical factors at the age of 7 were reported for the children in these legitimacy status groups, no detailed analysis of the relationship between any of these factors (including height) and other background circumstances was undertaken, although an analysis of height has been reported for the cohort as a whole (Davie *et al.*, 1972).

Height at 11

For this analysis we used the child's height at the age of 11 recorded during the medical examination carried out for the study (which was accompanied by precise instructions for making the measurement) rather than the more impressionistic assessment by teachers of the study child's height in comparison with his or her classmates, which was reported at 7 (Seglow *et al.*, 1972). Although the criterion used is different, adopted children were still found to be taller than illegitimate children at the age of 11 when no other factors were taken into account, but they were not significantly taller than legitimate children – see (b) in Table A12.1. Adopted children were, on average, likely to be 2.7cm taller than illegitimate children and about 1.5cm taller than legitimate children. It should be borne in mind, however, that the checks for biases in the sample (see Chapter 6) showed that somewhat fewer of the short children from a manual social class background in the adopted group at 7 responded at 11, so that adopted children, as a group, will appear slightly taller just for this reason. The difference in height between legitimate and illegitimate children was smaller, amounting to about 1.2cm, and was not significant.

When children of the same sex and social class background were compared, the difference in height between adopted and illegitimate children was no longer significant (Table S12.1). This means that although children who came from non-manual backgrounds were taller than children from manual backgrounds, an illegitimate child from a non-manual background was not likely to be significantly shorter than an adopted child or a legitimate child of the same background. Similarly there was no significant difference in the heights of children in the three legitimacy status groups when allowance was made only for the number of children in the household, or for whether the household was overcrowded, or for whether there was a child in the family receiving free school meals, although there was a slight difference when allowance was made for access to amenities only (Tables S12.2–5).

When all the factors were looked at together in the joint analysis, there were no significant differences in the height of children in the three legitimacy status groups who were living in similar circumstances (Table A12.1). Because there were differences in height between the groups, it is interesting to see where the differences lay when background circumstances were taken into account. Family size was clearly one of the most important influences when all the other factors had been taken into account, as children in small families were still likely to be 2.2cm taller, on average, than those in large families. Social class was also strongly related to differences in height, though our analysis shows that when all the other factors were taken into account the biggest differences (2.4cm) was between children with non-manual origins who were fatherless at 11 and those of manual origins who were fatherless at 11, regardless of whether their status was legitimate or illegitimate.

The relationship of height with factors such as family size, social class, overcrowding and free school meals, rather than with legitimacy status, remained when the family situation was examined (Table A12.2). Children from large families or those receiving free school meals were, for example, likely to be shorter than children from small families or those not receiving free school meals, and it made no significant difference whether they were, for instance, legitimate or illegitimate children living with both their own parents or living with step-parents. This was also the case for the adopted children, who were not likely to be taller than other children living in similar circumstances.

Thus the advantage in physical development displayed by adopted children, as measured by their height, could be attributed to the effects of living in a 'good environment' rather than to their adoptive status as such. Illegitimate children living in a similarly good environment were likely to be just as tall as adopted children. If they lived in a disadvantaged environment, and many illegitimate children were shown in this study to be in this situation, they were likely to be shorter than their more advantaged peers but probably as a result of factors such as overcrowded conditions, poverty or many mouths to feed rather than because they were born illegitimate.

13

School Attainment

Children's attainment at school has been the subject of an accumulating amount of research, which is well known. In particular the National Survey of Health and Development and the NCDS itself have documented the attainment of representative cohorts of children at regular intervals of time and also studied the children's relative progress between different ages (Douglas, 1964; Douglas *et al.*, 1968; Davie *et al.*, 1972; Fogelman and Goldstein, 1976). Although the children in both these cohorts were growing up in times when massive resources were being poured into education, and when strenuous attempts were being made to promote a more egalitarian society, the relevance and divisiveness of social factors have constantly been reiterated in the findings from these studies.

When the abilities of the adopted and illegitimate children were investigated at the age of 7, the adopted children were found to be better readers than either the legitimate or the illegitimate children; also they were as good at arithmetic as the legitimate children and better than the illegitimate (Crellin *et al.*, 1971; Seglow *et al.*, 1972). The results were considered to be very satisfactory for the adopted children, and to be evidence of disadvantage for the illegitimate.

Reading at 11

For the 11-year-old follow-up a test of reading comprehension constructed by the NFER to be parallel with the Watts–Vernon test was used in place of the Southgate reading test of word recognition (Southgate, 1962) used for the 7-year-old follow-up. The same procedure as at seven has been followed – relating differences between children's scores to years of 'reading age' by means of transforming the scores (see Appendix 1, and also Fogelman and Goldstein, 1976). It should be borne in mind that the differences in reading age which are reported here are related to this particular test, and to the independent variables in the analysis; and had another test or other variables been used, somewhat different results might have been obtained.

Although the reading test was different at 11, the unadjusted mean scores show that, as at 7, adopted children were more likely to be good readers than either the legitimate or the illegitimate children – see (b) in Table A13.1 (i). The adopted children were about 10 months ahead of the legitimate, who were, in turn, some 14 months ahead of the illegitimate children.

When the reading scores of children of the same sex and social class were examined, adopted children were still likely to be better readers, on average, than either legitimate or illegitimate children, even after allowance had been made for the very large differences between children living in non-manual and manual social class homes – see Table S13.1(i). In general, there was no difference in mean reading age between boys and girls, and as there was no significant interaction between sex, legitimacy status and reading, this suggests that at 11 both adopted boys and adopted girls were better at reading than the rest of the cohort. Although the differences were slightly reduced in each case, adopted children were also better readers on average than legitimate or illegitimate children when considering separately the relationship between reading test scores and family size, whether they were receiving free school meals or not, whether they were overcrowded, or whether they had access to amenities – see Table S13.2(i)–5(i). Even though children in small families were likely to be more than two years ahead in reading age than those in large families, adopted children were still, on average, a further 6 months ahead of legitimate children and 13 months ahead of illegitimate children. The difference in reading age between adopted children who were not overcrowded and legitimate or illegitimate children in similarly uncrowded homes was greater than this, and nearly as large as the unadjusted difference, but there was an interaction which showed that among those who were overcrowded there was no difference in reading attainment between children in the three legitimacy status groups. In every other case the illegitimate children were doing less well at reading than legitimate children.

It may come of something of a surprise, therefore, to see that, when all the variables were included in a joint analysis, there was no significant difference in reading age between the adopted, the legitimate and the illegitimate children – see Table A13.1(i). Clearly the combined effects of these environmental factors were more strongly related to children's reading at 11 than was their legitimacy status, and considering them in isolation can give an erroneous impression. That the adopted children may have been good readers, or illegitimate children poor readers, was related to the combination of home circumstances in which they lived, and their reading attainment was similar to that of legitimate children living in the same circumstances.

This finding made it important to see whether there were any differences in reading if the family situation was also examined. Children living with both adoptive parents might have been better readers than children living with step-parents, or illegitimate children living with their natural parents might have been poorer readers than legitimate children with both their own parents. When adopted children were compared with children in other family situations but *without* taking into account their home circumstances, they were significantly better readers than any of the others. Legitimate children living with both natural parents read better than legitimate children with step-parents or either of the two illegitimate groups. However, taking account of the family situation showed no difference in mean reading age among any of the groups of children *after* allowance had been made for the other factors in the analysis – see Table A13.2(i). This confirmed that environmental factors, taken together, were more strongly associated with the children's reading than legitimacy status, and they were also more strongly related than family situation, even when breaks had occurred in the family. The present analysis, which has considered all the illegitimate children, would seem to confirm Ferri's findings relating to illegitimate children in fatherless families, which she had regarded as tentative because the numbers were small (Ferri, 1976).

Reading progress between 7 and 11

A further question (see Chapter 11) was whether changes in reading ability had taken place in any of the legitimacy status groups between the ages of 7 and 11. If, for instance, adopted children living in similar circumstances at 11 had made less progress between 7 and 11 than children in such circumstances in the other two groups, or if the illegitimate children had made greater progress than other children living in similar background circumstances at 11, this might be one explanation for the lack of relationship between reading age and legitimacy status at 11. In fact, the analysis taking account of the children's 7-year reading score shows that there were no relative changes in reading ability between the groups between 7 and 11 years of age – see Table A13.3(i).

One of the implications of the results of the 11-year analyses of reading is the importance of the family's financial situation (measured in this study by the receipt of free school meals) and housing conditions (measured by crowding ratio and access to amenities). The analysis of the children's reading ability at 7 did not include them, and found significant differences between the legitimacy status groups (Crellin *et al.*, 1971); the analysis of 11-year scores and of changes between 7 and 11 carried out for present study did include them, and found no significant differences between the legitimacy status groups. This suggests that a consideration of income and housing factors in relation to children's reading is a vital element when comparing the ability and progress in this subject of adopted or illegitimate children.

Mathematics at 11

A test combining a mixture of problems and mechanical items constructed for the study by the NFER was used for the 11-year-old follow-up in place of the problem arithmetic test which was used at 7. A similar procedure was followed to that for the reading test, of converting raw scores to age equivalents. Again, as for reading, it should be borne in mind that the differences in mathematics age which are reported here are related to this particular test, and to the independent variables in the analysis; and had another test, or other variables, been used, different results might have been obtained.

The unadjusted means show adopted children doing very slightly (but not significantly) better on average at maths at 11 than legitimate children, while illegitimate children were about a year behind both these groups – see (b) in Table A13.1(ii). When the scores of children of the same sex and social class were examined, legitimate children were now doing very slightly better than the adopted, but the illegitimate children were still doing considerably worse than the other two groups – see Table S13.1(ii). In general, boys were likely to have slightly higher scores than girls after allowing for their social class, but there was a significant interaction between sex, legitimacy status and maths score. The estimated differences for this interaction revealed that there was only a small sex difference in maths attainment for legitimate children, but adopted girls scored considerably higher than adopted boys and also higher than legitimate boys, while illegitimate girls did noticeably worse than illegitimate boys and children in the other groups – see Table S13.1(ii). Evidence of a small association between sex and maths attainment among 11-year-olds but with no clear pattern has been noted in the cohort as a whole (Fogelman and Goldstein, 1976), and the present analysis appears to suggest that at least some of the differences may be associated with the children's legitimacy status.

The number of children in the household (family size) was another variable which did not show a straightforward relationship with legitimacy status and maths attainment. Although, on average, children from small families were 6 months ahead of those from middle-sized families and 16 months ahead of those from large ones, and legitimate children were likely to be another year ahead of illegitimate children, there was virtually no difference in maths ability between illegitimate children in middle- and large-sized families compared with the more evenly spaced difference between legitimate children in small, middle- and large-sized families – see Table S13.2(ii). When the relationship between maths scores and the receipt of free school meals, crowding and access to amenities were examined separately, adopted and legitimate children were, in each case, doing as well as each other and considerably better than illegitimate children, and there were no significant interactions between these variables and legitimacy status – see Table S13.3(ii)–5(ii).

The joint analysis of maths test scores, allowing for all these background factors, showed that there was no longer an interaction between legitimacy status and family size but there continued to be a significant interaction between legitimacy status, sex and maths score – see Table A13.1(ii). Whereas, in general, boys in the cohort showed slightly better maths attainment than girls, the adopted girls were, on average, doing better at maths than legitimate and adopted boys. The differences have been expressed diagrammatically in Figure 13.1. The two ends of each bar illustrate the approximate amount of difference between the extreme groups in the analysis *after* allowing for the other background factors included in the joint analysis. Thus it can be seen that, after allowing for their social class, family size and so on, adopted boys and adopted girls were at

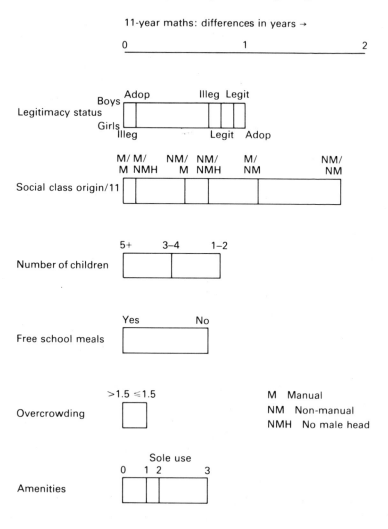

FIGURE 13.1   *Maths score and legitimacy status (AOV) – see also Table A13.1(ii)*

opposite ends of the bar. It can also be seen that legitimate boys had notably higher average scores than adopted boys, but the difference between legitimate and illegitimate boys was relatively small. Of all six groups, the adopted girls have the highest average score and the illegitimate girls the lowest.

In view of these findings we wondered if the family situation would throw some light on the differences. Before allowing for background circumstances the maths attainment of legitimate children living with both natural parents was significantly better than that of legitimate and illegitimate children living with step-parents and that of illegitimate children with both natural parents, but was not different to that of adopted children – see Table A13.2(ii). When background circumstances were allowed for, there was, again, a significant interaction between legitimacy status, family situation, sex and maths attainment – see Table A13.2(ii). Figure 13.2 shows that among the boys the adopted children had the lowest average maths scores, whereas adopted girls had the highest maths scores, but illegitimate girls living with both natural parents were the only ones to show significantly poorer maths attainment than that of legitimate children living with both natural parents. Quite why this should be must be a matter of speculation. There is some evidence to suggest that while mothers may have a greater influence on language development and reading ability (Davie *et al.*, 1972), fathers may have a greater influence on numerical skills (Carlsmith, 1964). It may, therefore, possibly be related to the fact that, although the family situations of these two groups appeared to be similar at the ages of 7 and 11, apart from legitimacy status, a number of the illegitimate children may not have had their father living in the family during the early years of their childhood; but we do not know whether this applied to girls more than boys. If fewer fathers of illegitimate girls were living in the families at the time these skills were being mastered, this might be one explanation for the difference between these two groups.

Despite experiencing changes in parenting, children in other of the family situations in our analysis (that is, legitimate step-family, adoptive, or illegitimate step-family) may have had or acquired father figures at a somewhat earlier age than some of the illegitimate girls who were now living with both their own parents. All but a handful of the adopted children, for instance, were known to have been placed in their adoptive homes by the age of two (Seglow *et al.*, 1972). If fathers do have an influence on maths attainment, one reason why adopted girls appeared to do unusually well at maths may be that their adoptive fathers may have taken a greater interest in developing this skill than most fathers. It is also possible that if adoptive fathers were experiencing role conflicts with their sons, or they still harboured a preference for a girl (see Chapters 5 and 8), these feelings could be reflected in adopted boys, on average, doing less well at maths than adopted girls.

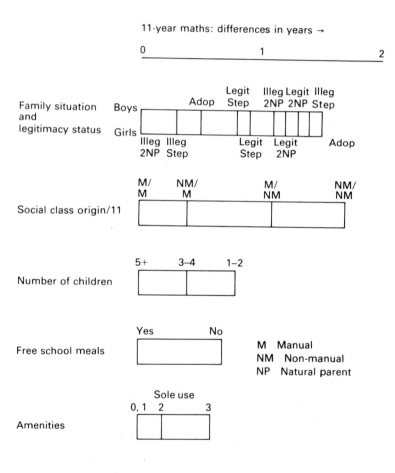

FIGURE 13.2   *Maths score and family situation (AOV) − see also Table A13.2(ii)*

Maths progress between 7 and 11

When the children's progress in maths ability between the ages of 7 and 11 was examined, it was clear that while adopted girls had progressed at a similar rate to legitimate girls living in similar home circumstances, adopted boys had made poorer progress in maths between the two ages than boys in either of the other two legitimacy status groups – see Table A13.3(ii). Illegitimate girls, on the other hand, made poorer progress at maths than illegitimate boys and also poorer progress than that of girls in the other two legitimacy status groups. Illegitimate boys had made as good progress at maths between 7 and 11 as legitimate boys living in similar home circumstances. The analysis showed that adopted children who had low scores at 7 were likely to make poorer progress than children with low scores in the other two legitimacy status groups and, in fact, illegitimate children with low scores at 7 made slightly better progress than low-scoring legitimate children. Although there were these differences in the rates of progress in maths ability between the ages of 7 and 11 between children who were legitimate and those who were adopted or illegitimate, they were relatively small. It is clear that the association between maths attainment and the other background variables in the analysis has contributed to the gap being small, although these factors do not explain all the differences between the legitimacy status groups.

14

Social Adjustment

Ratings of children's adjustment are coming increasingly to be seen as subjective and also, in many cases, as ephemeral (Rutter and Madge, 1976). But, however imperfect the measures and their interpretations, they represent a concern for an undeniable aspect of child development, namely, the child's ability to cope with and relate to people and situations in the world around him or her. Particularly with respect to adopted children there seems to be a fascination with behaviour traits and problems on the part of researchers and other writers, which probably reflects an anxiety on the part of parents and others concerned with the children to know whether they are 'turning out' all right. There seems to be an uncertainty as to whether difficulties might have occurred in any case, or have somehow been brought about by the special nature of the adoptive process (Jacka, 1973). For many of these reasons there is also an interest in the behaviour of illegitimate children who have not been adopted. In the present study we shall be confining our attention to the teacher's ratings of the child's adjustment in school.

When the children were 7 no difference in social adjustment was found between adopted and legitimate children, but illegitimate children were found to show a markedly higher degree of 'maladjusted' behaviour (Crellin *et al.*, 1971; Seglow *et al.*, 1972). The differences between legitimate and illegitimate children remained when certain background factors were taken into account, although social class and sex differences appeared to have a greater relationship with the children's social adjustment than their legitimacy status. When these two factors were examined more closely, they indicated that adopted boys, and especially those being brought up in middle-class homes, were more prone to be maladjusted than either adopted girls or boys from the whole cohort.

Social adjustment at 11

The Bristol Social Adjustment Guide (BSAG), which had been used at 7, was also used at 11 to assess the child's adjustment in school. This instrument has been fully described elsewhere but, briefly, it contains some 250 descriptions of behaviour, and teachers were asked to underline those which 'best fit' the child in question (Stott, 1966). A coding system accompanies the Guide and the summation of particular items indicates the child's level of adjustment; the higher the score, the poorer the adjustment. For this study the scores have been transformed for use as a continuous dependent variable in the analyses of variance and are, therefore, described in terms of ranging from 'poor' to 'good' adjustment instead of using Stott's three categories of 'stable', 'unsettled' or 'maladjusted'.

At 11 the unadjusted means revealed that the illegitimate children were again reported by their teachers to show. poorer social adjustment than legitimate children – see (b) in Table A14.1. The behaviour of the adopted children came in between these two groups but was not significantly different from either that of legitimate or of illegitimate children. When the social adjustment of children of similar sex and social class backgrounds was compared, the adopted children were found to be no different to illegitimate children (Table S14.1). Children living in non-manual social class homes at 11 showed better adjustment than those living in manual homes, and the least well adjusted were children in families with no male head of household who came from a manual social class of origin. After allowing for these social class differences boys were still significantly less well adjusted than girls, but the tendency for adopted girls to be as well adjusted as legitimate girls at 7 (Seglow *et al.*, 1972) did not appear at 11. Family size was another factor which appeared to be associated with an increase in the difference in social adjustment between adopted and legitimate children, so that, although children in small families were likely to be better adjusted on average than children in large families, adopted children in small families were said to be less well adjusted than legitimate children in small families and no better adjusted than illegitimate children in small families (Table S14.2). Among those receiving free school meals there were few adopted children, but they were likely to be as poorly adjusted as the illegitimate children (Table S14.3). Conversely, illegitimate children not in receipt of free school meals were as well adjusted as adopted children not receiving free meals. When the relationship between social adjustment and overcrowding or access to amenities was considered separately, adopted children, although somewhat less well adjusted, were not significantly different in this respect to legitimate children living in similar housing conditions, but illegitimate children were considered relatively poorly adjusted (Tables S14.4–5).

The separate analyses indicated that although the difference in social adjustment between illegitimate and legitimate children was only slightly reduced when allowance was made for background circumstances, these were accounting for a considerable difference as far as the adopted children were concerned. This was confirmed by the joint analysis, which showed that, when all the factors were taken into consideration, adopted children as well as illegitimate children were significantly less well adjusted on average than legitimate children in similar home circumstances (Table A14.1 and Figure 14.1). There was an exception to this general pattern in that adopted children living in small families, but not illegitimate children in small families, were likely to be less well adjusted than legitimate children living in small families and otherwise similar home circumstances. If the family situation was also taken into consideration, would the adjustment of adopted children still continue, on average, to be more like that of legitimate children, or might it come somewhere in between?

Once again, the answer to this question depends on whether or not related background circumstances are taken into account. If they are not, adopted children do come somewhere in the middle as having adjustment similar to legitimate children living with step-parents. Such children were less well adjusted than legitimate children living with both their own parents at 7 and 11. But they were considerably better adjusted than illegitimate children living with step-parents (Table A14.2). However, when the other background factors were included in the analysis, adopted children were slightly (but not significantly) less well adjusted than illegitimate children living with both their own parents, and only the illegitimate children living with step-parents showed poorer adjustment (Figure 14.2). The relatively poor adjustment of the adopted children persisted despite the

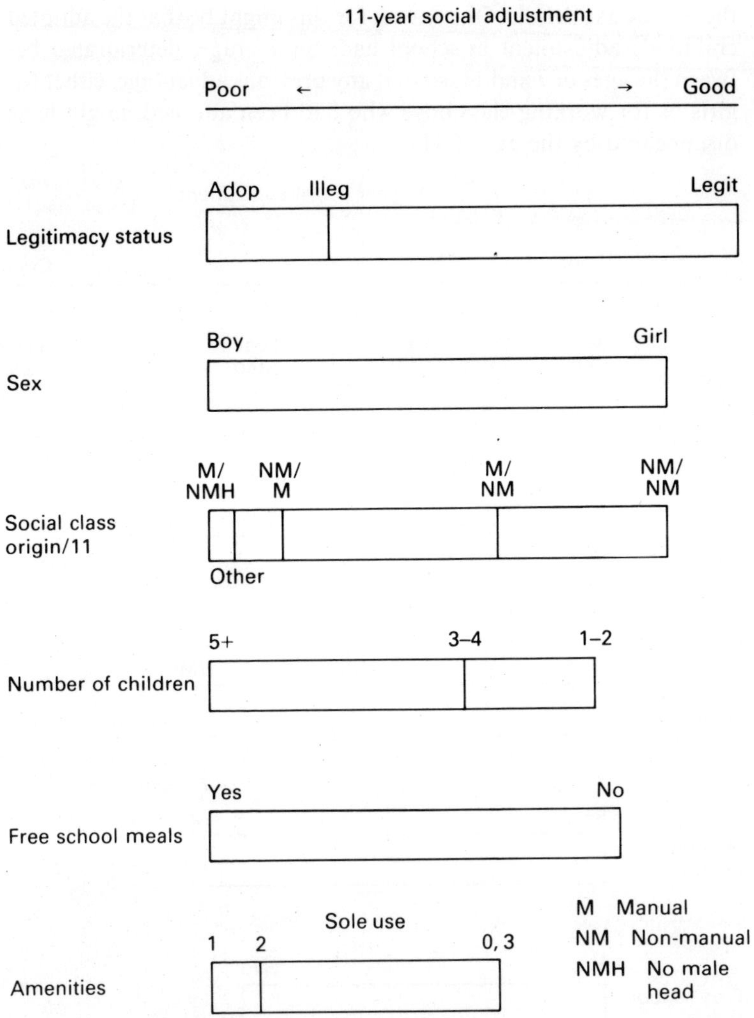

11-year social adjustment

FIGURE 14.1   *Social adjustment and legitimacy status (AOV) — see also Table A14.1*

considerable advantage that many of them would have gained from living in a non-manual social class home at 11. There were no differences in this respect between adopted boys and girls, as there had been at 7; thus at 11 there appeared to be no reversal as far as sex or social class were concerned among the adopted to the trends for the cohort as a whole. One reason for this might be that the adopted children's adjustment in school had, on average, deteriorated between the ages of 7 and 11, so that any previous advantage, either for girls or for working-class boys who had been adopted, might have disappeared by the age of 11.

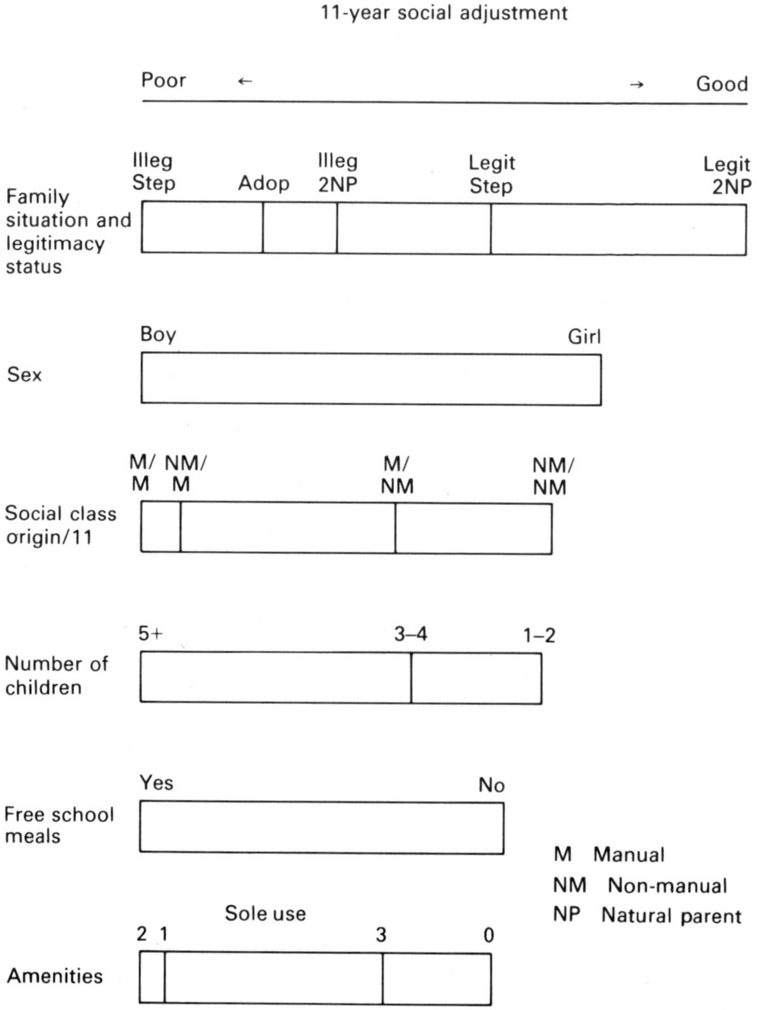

11-year social adjustment

FIGURE 14.2   *Social adjustment and family situation (AOV) – see also Table A14.2*

Changes between 7 and 11

When changes between 7 and 11 in adjustment to school were examined, it did appear to be the case that the behaviour of the adopted children had deteriorated significantly in comparison with that of legitimate children during these four years, when related home circumstances were taken into account (Table A14.3). In terms of changes in behaviour the illegitimate children had not done so well as legitimate children, but they had done considerably better, on average, than the adopted children.

Clearly environmental factors are an important consideration when looking at the adjustment to school of adopted or illegitimate children, but for varying reasons. In the case of illegitimate children they demonstrate that differences between their behaviour and that of adopted children may be explained by their home circumstances, and although these home circumstances do not account for all the difference between illegitimate and legitimate children, they reduce it. In the case of adopted children environmental factors, particularly if they are ones which most people would consider privileged (such as non-manual social class), may mask problems of adjustment which are nevertheless a matter of concern to their teachers. Some of the possible interpretations will be discussed in the overview in Chapter 16, and in the final chapter, which discusses the importance of birth status.

Part IV

Fitting the Patterns Together

15
Summary of Main Findings

A large amount of data has been presented in the last eight chapters. We thought it might be helpful to readers to make a summary in note form at this point, bringing together and highlighting the main findings. This might also be useful to those who wish to read the findings quickly and in shorter form. Readers may, however, prefer to skip this chapter altogether and move to the overview in Chapter 16.

The sample at 11 (Chapter 6)

Illegitimate	N = 294
Legitimate	N = 12 076
Adopted (born illegitimate)	N = 115

The adopted group consists of illegitimate children adopted by two people, neither of whom is a natural parent. Children adopted into step-families (that is, with one natural parent) or by a lone parent are contained within the other two groups, depending on their birth status. Legitimately born children who were adopted before the age of 7 by two people, neither of them a natural parent, have been excluded from the sample.

Parental care at 11 (Chapter 7)

Children living in two-parent situations: illegitimate 66 per cent, adopted 93 per cent, legitimate 94 per cent. Two-parent situations have been defined as those where the child currently lives either with both natural parents, with one natural and one step/adoptive parent, or with two adoptive parents.

Children living with a lone (natural) parent: illegitimate 21 per cent, adopted 0 per cent, legitimate 5 per cent.

Children ever in care: illegitimate 16 per cent, legitimate 3 per cent, adopted, not certain.

Changes in parental-care situation between the ages of 7 and 11 showed that at least 14 per cent of illegitimate children, compared with at least 5 per cent of legitimate children, were living in different family situations at 11 to the ones they had been in at 7. Of the children who lived with both their natural parents at 7, 91 per cent of the illegitimate were also living with them at 11, compared with 96 per cent of the legitimate. Only 4 per cent of the adopted children living with both adoptive parents at 7 had experienced a change in family situation by the age of 11.

Social class at 11 (Chapter 8)

Non-manual: illegitimate 12 per cent, adopted 60 per cent, legitimate 34 per cent.

Adopted children in non-manual homes at 7 remained, with very few exceptions, in a middle-class background, and 22 per cent of those in manual homes at 7 moved into non-manual homes between the ages of 7 and 11. Half the illegitimate children who were living in a non-manual background at 7 were in manual or no male head situations at 11, compared with 14 per cent of legitimate children.

Comparisons between the social class background of the children's natural mother (social class of origin) and the children's social class at 11 showed that only 23 per cent of the illegitimate children with a non-manual social class of origin were also non-manual at 11, compared with 78 per cent of the adopted and 57 per cent of the legitimate children.

Sex (Chapter 8)

Boys: illegitimate 42 per cent, adopted 57 per cent, legitimate 51 per cent.

The distribution at 11 was similar to that at 7 and showed no social class differences. The ratio of boys to girls was significantly lower among the illegitimate than among the legitimate or the adopted.

Family size at 11 (Chapter 8)

Small families (1–2 children aged under 21 in household): illegitimate 43 per cent, adopted 79 per cent, legitimate 44 per cent.

Adopted children were more often the only child in the household than children in the other two groups. Differences in family size were associated with social class as well as legitimacy status except within the adopted group.

Natural parents with large families (5 + children aged under 21 in household): illegitimate 30 per cent, legitimate 15 per cent.

The family size of illegitimate and legitimate children living with step-parents showed no significant differences, but there was a tendency for a higher proportion of illegitimate than legitimate children in fatherless families to be living in small-sized families.

Families on low incomes at 11 (Chapter 9)

Families receiving supplementary benefit and/or free school meals: illegitimate 33 per cent, adopted 4 per cent, legitimate 13 per cent.

Natural parents receiving neither benefit: illegitimate 71 per cent, legitimate 90 per cent.

Among children in step-families or fatherless families there were no significant differences between the illegitimate and the legitimate in the proportion who were receiving either benefit.

Crowding at 11 (Chapter 10)

Overcrowded (more than 1.5 persons per rom): illegitimate 16 per cent, adopted 3 per cent, legitimate 11 per cent.

Among those living with their natural parents, 24 per cent of the illegitimate children, compared with 11 per cent of the legitimate, were overcrowded. There were no significant differences in the proportion of illegitimate and legitimate children living in step-families or in fatherless families who were overcrowded.

Overcrowded at either 7 and/or 11: illegitimate 27 per cent, adopted 8 per cent, legitimate 17 per cent.

The proportion of illegitimate children (11 per cent) and of legitimate children (8 per cent) who were living in overcrowded conditions at both ages was not significantly different.

Amenities at 11 (Chapter 10)

Sole use of indoor toilet, bathroom and hot water: illegitimate 74 per cent, adopted 97 per cent, legitimate 88 per cent.

In all, 10 per cent of illegitimate children either shared all three or had none of these amenities, compared with 3 per cent of legitimate children. Illegitimate children living with natural parents and in fatherless families were more likely to share or have no amenities than legitimate children in these parental situations. Among children living with step-parents there was no significant difference in access to amenities between illegitimate and legitimate children.

Lacking one or more amenities at either 7 and/or 11: illegitimate 43 per cent, adopted 6 per cent, legitimate 20 per cent.

Tenure at 11 (Chapter 10)

Living in owner-occupied homes: illegitimate 26 per cent, adopted 65 per cent, legitimate 46 per cent.

Illegitimate children living in owned houses at 7 were less likely than legitimate children still to be living in them at 11. The great majority of illegitimate and legitimate children living in council housing at 7 were still in such housing at 11. Over 50 per cent of illegitimate and legitimate children living in private rented homes at seven had moved to other forms of tenure by the age of 11.

Natural parents living in owned tenure: illegitimate 32 per cent, legitimate 47 per cent.

Among children with step-parents there were no significant differences in tenure according to whether they were illegitimate or legitimate, but only 12 per cent of illegitimate children in fatherless families were in owned homes, compared with 27 per cent of legitimate children in fatherless families.

Height at 11 (Chapter 12)

For a full description of the methods of analysis of the developmental outcomes, please see Chapter 11. Descriptions of the measures used can be found in the relevant chapters.
(1) Legitimacy status: unadjusted differences showed that adopted children were significantly taller ($p < .05$) than illegitimate children, but they were not taller than legitimate children. There

was no significant difference in height between illegitimate and legitimate children.

Adjusted differences after allowing for all the other independent variables (see Chapter 11): none.

(2) Family situation: there were no differences according to family situation. The small difference in height between adopted and illegitimate children was clearly related to environmental factors rather than to legitimacy status.

Reading at 11 (Chapter 13)

(1) Legitimacy status: unadjusted differences showed that adopted children were better readers than illegitimate children ($p < .001$) and legitimate children ($p < .05$).

Adjusted differences: none.

(2) Family situation – unadjusted scores: children with both adoptive parents were better readers than children in all the other groups ($p < .001$). When compared only with legitimate children with two natural parents, they still read better ($p < .05$). Legitimate children with two natural parents were better readers than legitimate children with step-parents ($p < .01$) and better than illegitimate children with two natural parents ($p < .001$) or with step-parents ($p < .01$).

Adjusted differences: none.

(3) Changes between 7 and 11: no change in relative levels of reading attainment.

The differences in reading between adopted children and those in other legitimacy status groups or other family situations were associated with advantageous environmental conditions. Housing and financial aspects were important factors in this analysis.

Mathematics at 11 (Chapter 13)

(1) Legitimacy status: unadjusted differences showed that adopted children did as well at maths as legitimate children and significantly better than illegitimate children ($p < .001$). There was a tendency ($p < .05$) for adopted boys to do less well at maths than those in the other legitimacy status groups, and for adopted children in medium-sized families (3–4 children) to do less well

than legitimate children but about the same as illegitimate children.

Adjusted differences: adopted boys continued to do less well at maths ($p < .05$) than boys in the other two legitimacy status groups, and illegitimate girls did less well than legitimate or adopted girls ($p < .05$). Family size no longer showed a difference with respect to legitimacy status.

(2) Family situation: the unadjusted scores showed children with both adoptive parents doing as well as legitimate children with two natural parents. Children in all the other parental situations were doing less well than legitimate children with two natural parents, and those doing worst of all ($p < .001$) were illegitimate children with two natural parents.

Adjusted scores: only the illegitimate girls living with both natural parents were significantly different ($p < .001$) from legitimate children with two natural parents. Adoptive boys were doing less well ($p < .05$) than boys in any of the other groups, but illegitimate boys living with step-parents were doing as well at maths as legitimate boys with both natural parents.

(3) Changes between 7 and 11: these showed that adopted children, and adopted boys in particular, did not progress as well between 7 and 11 as legitimate children when other factors were allowed for. Illegitimate boys, on the other hand, had made similar progress to legitimate boys between 7 and 11.

When family and environmental factors were taken into account, only illegitimate girls living with both their own parents and adopted boys were doing less well at maths than other children.

Social adjustment in school at 11 (Chapter 14)

(1) Legitimacy status: unadjusted differences revealed that illegitimate children showed poorer adjustment ($p < .01$) than legitimate children, but they were not more poorly adjusted than adopted children.

Adjusted differences: both illegitimate and adopted children showed significantly poorer adjustment ($p < .001$) than legitimate children. In small families (one or two children) the adopted children tended to show poorer behaviour than the illegitimate children ($p < .05$). There were no interactions between legitimacy status, social adjustment and sex or social class.

(2) Family situation: unadjusted differences revealed that legitimate children living with two natural parents showed better adjustment than children in any of the other groups, the poorest ($p < .001$) being illegitimate children living with step-parents.

Adjusted differences: there was no longer a difference between legitimate children who were with both parents and those with step-parents, but children living with both adoptive parents and illegitimate children showed poorer adjustment.

(3) Changes between 7 and 11: the social adjustment of the adopted children deteriorated significantly ($p < .001$), compared with that of legitimate children. The relative adjustment of the illegitimate children did not show such a noticeable change between 7 and 11.

The social adjustment at 11 of adopted children did not differ from that of illegitimate children, and, taking family and environmental circumstances into account, showed a significant difference in social adjustment between both adopted and illegitimate children and those who were legitimately born. Thus, when allowance was made for their relatively favourable physical environment, adopted children were as liable as illegitimate children to be considered to be showing behaviour difficulties at school.

16

Overview

Family and environmental circumstances

The illegitimate children

It is very clear from a study of the circumstances of each parental situation that illegitimate children are not a homogeneous group. Among them there are differences according to whether the children were living at the age of 11 with both their own parents, with one natural parent (usually their mother) and one step-parent or adoptive parent, with a lone parent, or with a variety of caretakers (including being in care) in 'other situations'. When the circumstances of the legitimate children in similar parental situations are compared with those of the illegitimate, there are, in some cases, few if any differences according to legitimacy status.

As a group, the illegitimate children who had not been adopted were in very many respects living in social circumstances at the age of 11 different to those who had been adopted and to legitimately born children. One out of every three illegitimate children was living with a lone parent or in 'other situations', and one in six had been in care at some time. Only one in eight had fathers (or father-substitutes) with non-manual occupations, and one in three of the families was receiving state benefits. Only one in four came from families who owned their houses, and one in seven lived in the private rented sector. One in six was living in overcrowded conditions, and one in four lived in accommodation which lacked at least one basic amenity.

Wedge and Prosser (1973) have illustrated vividly the disadvantages that accompany an accumulation of some of these situations (one parent, receiving state benefits, poor housing). But even if only a proportion fall into this extreme group a disturbingly high percentage of illegitimate children are growing up in conditions that compare unfavourably with those of other children.

However, it needs to be emphasised that although illegitimate children were more likely to be living in unfavourable conditions, they were *not* all living in them. There were children with fathers in non-manual occupations, two-thirds were not receiving supplementary benefit or free school meals, one in four lived in owner-occupied housing at 11, three out of four were in families with sole use of all basic amenities, five out of six were not overcrowded, and five out of six had never been in care. Thus the majority of illegitimate children were living in an environment where material conditions were reasonably good, although they were less likely to be stable than for legitimate or adopted children.

Two out of every five of the illegitimate children were living with both their own parents at the age of 11, and when their circumstances were compared with those of legitimate children living with both their own parents, the illegitimate were in many respects living in poorer circumstances. They were more likely than legitimate children to be living in families receiving state benefits, more likely to be overcrowded, and more likely to be sharing or lacking amenities. A higher proportion of illegitimate children living with both natural parents were in large families, and this would be associated with the receipt of free school meals and with overcrowding. This explanation, though, does nothing to diminish the relatively greater hardships experienced by these illegitimate children. If anything, it highlights them. The study did not ask couples if they were married to each other, but some of the hardships experienced by illegitimate children living with both their own parents may be related to more frequent ambiguities in their parents' marital status, which may have put their parents in a weaker position for obtaining, for example, reasonable housing. Although, in some respects, these children may have been fortunate to be looked after by their own parents, some of them may have suffered a double stigma from their own illegitimacy and from attitudes to their parents' marital status. That this may be the case is also suggested by the situation of illegitimate children living in step-families.

Legitimate children in step-families were likely to be living in very similar circumstances to illegitimate children, and poorer circumstances than legitimate children with both their own parents. For many illegitimate and legitimate children these reconstituted families will have represented the end of a lone-parent situation; more noticeably than for any of the other groups the pathways of care seemed to converge to the point where birth status no longer made a difference to the material circumstances. No significant differences were found in family size, in the proportions ever in care, in the proportions receiving state benefits, in the proportions living in overcrowded conditions, or in those sharing or lacking amenities. As far as these material conditions went, living in a step-family appeared to provide the 'best' chance for illegitimate children.

The circumstances of children living with a lone mother at the age of 11 did, however, reflect the different pathways to this situation. Although, for example, there was no difference in the high proportions of legitimate or illegitimate children living in fatherless families who were in receipt of state benefits at the time of the study, the fact that most illegitimate children had not had the benefit of a matrimonial home showed up in their housing conditions. Fewer illegitimate children were living in owner-occupied homes, and more of them shared or lacked household amenities. There was a tendency for illegitimate children in fatherless families to be in small families (or to be an only child) more often than legitimate children. A higher proportion of illegitimate children had also been in care at some time. When measured by factors such as receipt of benefits, living in rented accommodation, and lack of amenities, the circumstances of fatherless children were worse than those of children, whether legitimate or illegitimate, in any of the other parental situations, as Ferri (1976) has so clearly demonstrated.

The group of children in 'other situations' were living with such a variety of caretakers that it would be unwise to discuss their circumstances as a group. But we may note that one in three of both the legitimate and the illegitimate children in these 'other situations' had been (or were still) in care, and that the illegitimate children tended to be living in small-sized families at 11.

It has already been noted that one in every seven of the illegitimate children experienced a change in parental situation between the ages of 7 and 11, compared with one in every twenty of the legitimate children. The effects of such changes are reflected in the proportions who were living in different social class backgrounds and in different forms of tenure at each age. In both instances the changes for the illegitimate children tended to be towards downward rather than upward social mobility, and out of owner-occupied housing rather than into it, in reverse of the pattern of change for legitimate children. One in four illegitimate children had lived in overcrowded conditions at 7 and at 11, and over two in every five had had to share amenities or do without them at one or other age. The sheer practical complications of such a high degree of change and deprivation within four years, let alone the emotional consequences, must have been considerable. Wilson and Herbert (1978) have drawn a vivid picture of the adaptability and the dangers which result from the pressures experienced by families living in broadly similar circumstances to those of many of the illegitimate children.

The adopted children

In every respect the illegitimately born children who had been adopted by the age of 7 were, as a group, continuing to live in exceptionally favourable circumstances at 11. Very few of them had experienced a break in the family between the ages of 7 and 11. Three out of every five had adoptive fathers with non-manual occupations and the financial situation in the families was such that only 4 per cent reported receiving state benefits. Four out of every five were growing up in small families, with the greater access to resources and parental attention that this was likely to bring. Two out of every three lived in owner-occupied homes, and almost all the adopted children were exceptionally well off in terms of space and amenities.

The great majority of adopted children had experienced no changes in their environmental conditions between the ages of 7 and 11. Where there had been changes during these four years, they were more often from manual to non-manual social class, from council housing to owner-occupied, from lack of amenities to sole use of all three, rather than the reverse.

The authors of *Growing-up Adopted* suggested that these very favourable conditions were due, to some extent, 'to the very rigorous selection procedures which are generally applied by adoption agencies prior to placing a child' (Seglow *et al.*, 1972). It is notable that the adoptive families were able to maintain or even to improve these conditions during 11 years of the children's lives. This was not simply a feature of middle-class standards, as the children living in a working-class background also enjoyed very high material standards. One reason for this probably lies in the predominantly small size of the adoptive families, which meant that with fewer to feed, clothe and care for, it was easier to maintain, or attain, high material standards. Although some of the families were known to contain a mixture of own and adoptive children, the smaller families could be said to be a feature of their adoptive state. In and around 1958 adoption agencies tended to 'ration' children to give more couples the chance of having one, and, with some exceptions, they also tended not to make placements where there were already several natural children. Another possible reason is that, as the adoptive parents were, on average, older than parents in the other two legitimacy status groups, they would have been likely to be more settled in their jobs and further up promotion ladders, as well as having had longer to acquire such things as a well-equipped house.

When the situations of the adopted and the illegitimate children at 11 are compared, it is very hard to believe that these two groups of children apparently had potentially equal chances at birth (Seglow *et al.*, 1972). Adoption has undoubtedly provided a form of parental care which has given one group an environment vastly different to that of a considerable proportion of the other group.

Developmental outcomes

The illegitimate children

The need to take account of family and environmental factors when looking at measures of child development is forcibly brought home by a comparison of the unadjusted and the adjusted scores of the illegitimate children. On the face of it there was only one characteristic, out of the four examined, which did not single them out from legitimately born 11-year-olds, and that was their height. At school both their attainment, as measured by reading and maths, and their social adjustment appeared to be poorer than that of legitimate children. When compared with adopted children, there was, again, only one characteristic in which the illegitimate children did not appear to be worse off, and that was social adjustment.

But when social class, sex, family size, housing and financial differences were taken into account, there was a considerable change in this picture. The most dramatic was that there was no longer a difference in their reading ability at 11 compared with that of legitimate or adopted children. Nor were there any differences in height. When family situation was considered in greater detail, only the illegitimate girls living with both their natural parents were still doing significantly less well in maths, while illegitimate boys were doing just as well at maths as legitimate boys and better than adopted boys.

However, although the differences between illegitimate and legitimate children's social adjustment at school were reduced by family and environmental factors, they were still significant. Exactly why this was so must to some extent be a matter of conjecture, but for one reason or another the fact that teachers rated illegitimate children as showing, on average, poor social adjustment could not be explained by our measures of their relatively poorer home circumstances. Both before and after adjusting for environmental circumstances, illegitimate children living with both natural parents (who tended to live in more disadvantaged surroundings) were rated as somewhat better adjusted than illegitimate children with step-parents. It is possible that children who knew they were living with their own mother and father (whatever their precise marital situation) felt more secure than children living with a step-parent, although their illegitimate birth status still appeared to give rise to difficulties.

Another factor which may have been important as far as social adjustment was concerned, but which was not included in the analyses of variance (apart from changes in social class between birth and eleven), was the effect of the greater number of changes in background circumstances experienced by illegitimate children. Descriptive reference has been made in this study to the amount of changes experienced by these children between the ages of 7 and 11, measured at just two points in time. They suggest that even higher proportions of children will have experienced changes in the first 7 years of life and at times in between the ages of 7 and 11 (Crellin *et al.*, 1971, refer, for example, to more moves and changes of school and more absenteeism among illegitimate children). Constant change is a well-known stress factor, and this is linked with both anxiety and aggression and with difficulties in forming relationships, all of which were types of behaviour included in the measure of social adjustment.

If this is so, it makes it all the more remarkable that the illegitimate children were reading at 11 as well as their peers and mostly doing as well at maths, as learning difficulties are often thought to run parallel with emotional or behavioural difficulties (Rutter and Madge, 1976). It is also interesting that there were no differences in height, as stress, particularly in early childhood, has been linked with stunted physical growth (Rutter and Madge, 1976). There are likely to have been some illegitimate children who experienced such problems, just as there will have been others doing exceptionally well, but the general picture suggests that the illegitimate children were making very satisfactory progress at the age of 11 in view of all the adverse circumstances which had been affecting their lives.

It is also important to note that, when environmental factors were taken into account, there were no significant differences between illegitimate and adopted children. As far as height and school attainment were concerned, the disadvantages of being illegitimate rather than adopted appeared to have been wholly due to less favourable environmental circumstances rather than to legitimacy status as such. With regard to social adjustment, it would seem likely that other factors besides environmental ones were at work.

In these analyses we included a composite measure of social class which enabled us to see whether it made a significant difference to the results at 11 if children in the three legitimacy status groups had, for example, been born into a middle-class background but were, at 11, living in a working-class family or one with no male head of household. The finding showed that children who were born to mothers with a middle-class background and were living at 11 in middle-class homes had a clear advantage over children who were in working-class homes at both ages. On the other hand children who lived in a middle-class home at one age but not the other came, as one might expect, somewhere in between the extremes. However, this pattern held constant, irrespective of the child's legitimacy status. Thus, the overall results are not explained by any exceptional progress of illegitimate children who at 11 were living in manual homes (or with no male head of household) but whose mothers were of non-manual social class of origin. Conversely, adopted children who were born to mothers with a manual social class of origin, but who were at 11 living in non-manual homes, were doing no better than legitimate or illegitimate children who had become upwardly mobile in their social class background.

The adopted children

The unadjusted scores showed that adopted children, as a group, were doing very well indeed at 11. They were reading significantly better than legitimate children, they were doing just as well at maths, their social adjustment was no worse, and, although not significantly so, they were slightly taller. No one would deny that for a group of children with an uncertain start in life this was a considerable achievement. But it must be set within the context of the exceptionally favourable environmental circumstances in which these children were living. When this was done, the advantages were seen to be associated with them rather than with their adoptive status as such. They shared their good development with other middle-class children, with other small families, with other well-housed or financially secure families; or, if they lived in working-class homes, in larger families, in poorer housing or financial circumstances, they did not have an advantage from being adopted. In the case of maths, for example, adopted boys were doing rather worse than others.

The finding of most importance and concern is that when such factors were taken into account, adopted children's social adjustment was poorer than that of legitimate children, and showed signs of having deteriorated relative to that of other children since the age of 7. Many concerned with adoption will not find this surprising. There were already indications at 7 that some of the adopted children were more prone to behaviour difficulties than legitimate children (Seglow *et al.*, 1972). Most of them knew by then about their adoption and by the age of 11 even fewer (if any) of them would have been ignorant of this fact, even if the conjoint fact (in these particular children's case) of their illegitimacy had not been made very explicit. Many of them would have been starting to adjust to the knowledge that their adoptive parents were not their natural parents and coming to terms with their own identity. Much has been written about the preparatory work which goes on for all children during the apparently emotionally quieter period leading up to adolescence and before the full-blown explosions of that period (Rapoport *et al.*, 1977). By the age of 11, too, at least some of the girls and a few boys would have been pubescent. Coming to terms with their adoptive status would, then, have been an added factor for this group.

The same attention which led to the adoptive parents providing such excellent physical care is likely to have spread to the children's emotional development, but there may, nevertheless, have been some strains and conflicts. Both the interest and the possible conflicts may, in turn, have come, or been brought, to the teachers' attention, so that they may have been reporting the adopted children's behaviour in a somewhat different way to that of other children. Another factor, as far as some of the adoptive parents were concerned, may have been an exaggerated uncertainty about their own reactions and responses which had communicated itself to the children and made relationships harder for them. There was some support for this suggestion in our finding that the social adjustment of adopted children from small families was poorer than that of other children from small families. It is possible, too, that the adopted children found it easier to be naughty at school than at home and used school as a safety valve. Tizard (1977) found that teachers rated adopted children as having more behaviour problems than those in her comparison groups. Other studies (Bohman, 1971; Raynor, 1980) have suggested that adopted children tend to show behaviour problems in mid-childhood which are later resolved. It will, therefore, be of great interest to study the behaviour of this same group later in life.

17
Does Birth Status Matter?

In the main, *Born Illegitimate* (Crellin *et al.*, 1971) and *Growing-up Adopted* (Seglow *et al.*, 1972) encompassed the first 7 years of these children's lives (and beyond, in many respects, for the latter), and posed a number of questions related to two central issues: 'Is illegitimacy still a problem?' and 'How do adopted children make out?' They were able to give some answers regarding the children's early experiences and their progress up to the age of 7, but other questions could be answered only partially in view of their longitudinal nature.

The present report takes the story along another four years and provides information about the children's development at 11, but it, in turn, must leave some questions unanswered. Even a study of the data collected when these children are 16 will not be able to give final answers, and it has been argued that 'the crucial test of how well we have succeeded as parents, as teachers and as a society in caring for our young is how they themselves make out as parents, citizens and workers' (Crellin *et al.*, 1971). Some would say that we can never tell how things have gone in any final sense while people are still alive, and life is full of surprises.

In combining the two previously parallel studies into one in this report a central question has been, 'Does birth status matter?' In seeking some answers we have looked particularly carefully at the children's family (parental-care) situation, at certain environmental characteristics and at certain developmental outcomes, and at the interrelationships between these factors, one with another and together with their birth status.

There are, of course, many other aspects which are relevant to the issue of birth status, but which have not been covered in this report.

Some personal or environmental characteristics, on which information was available from the NCDS, could perhaps have been included, but would have been more difficult to interpret. Others would have required the collection of additional data, such as that collected on the adopted children separately from the main follow-up at 7 and reported in *Growing-up Adopted*. Still others would have required an entirely different type of study from this essentially large-scale and longitudinal work.

One such aspect is the quality of relationships between parents and children. This is not an easy subject to monitor and would have been particularly complicated when children of different legitimacy status and with different parental caretakers were being considered. Studies such as those conducted by the Newsons (e.g. Newson and Newson, 1963), which use very detailed interview techniques, or direct observational studies (e.g. Ainsworth, 1964), would seem to be more appropriate for this particular aspect.

Family situation

When current theories about the family (see Chapter 3) have been matched against the reality of demographic facts, the discrepancy between the ideal of the conventional nuclear family and the actual diversity of family life has been obvious. While it is true that the majority of children continue to live with both their own parents, the rates of separation and divorce are such that increasing proportions of families are broken, for a time at least, and many are then reconstituted following remarriage. Gill (1977) has pointed out that the pathways of care for legitimate children are towards fatherlessness while those for illegitimate children are away from it. This pattern, and the resulting diversity of family life, is apparent when the parental-care situations at the age of 11 of the children in the present study are examined.

One in ten of the legitimate children were no longer living in an unbroken family consisting of both natural parents. Two out of five of the illegitimate children were living with both natural parents, and altogether two-thirds of the illegitimate children were in two-parent families. Although a higher proportion of illegitimate than legitimate children were living in one-parent families at the age of 11, Ferri (1976) has shown that as a proportion of all children in one-parent families, illegitimate children formed only 8 per cent of the total. It is true that illegitimate children were more likely to change their parental situation than legitimate children, but once they were no longer living with both natural parents, legitimate children also tended to change situations between 7 and 11. Some would say that none, rather than five, of the adopted children should have experienced a break in their family between the ages of 7 and 11, but most of the adopted children continued to live in the same parental situation, which to all outward appearances resembled the conventional model of mother and father married to each other.

The fact that by the age of 11 so many of the children who were illegitimately born were living in families which resembled the norm, at least in outward terms, raises the question, 'Is birth status only important as far as family situation is concerned at the time of birth rather than as a continuing factor?' At birth, if the child was illegitimate, there was something about him or her (that is, lack of legitimate status) and the family into which he or she was born (that is, lack of legal marriage of the natural parents) which made their experience different to that of the legitimately born and often resulted in an uncertain period for the mother while she coped alone or decided to part with her child for adoption. Those who were then adopted acquired both a new mother and a new father who were married to each other and became their legal parents when the adoption order was granted. Many of the rest of the illegitimately born children were legitimated by the marriage of their own parents or were adopted by their step-parents to formalise the situation. Legitimate children whose families broke up were sharing the experience of living with a lone parent or of acquiring a step-parent. So neither marriage nor togetherness was the prerogative of one birth status against the other once the children started to grow up, and as the years go by the lines have converged, crossed and criss-crossed, so that the type of parental-care situation becomes less important than the quality of care within it.

Environmental characteristics

The advantages and disadvantages of factors such as social class, family size, income and housing, and the way they tend to interact and reinforce each other, are well known (Chapter 2). Often they seem to lead to a split between 'middle-class' and 'working-class' families. Extremes of disadvantages can lead to a 'culture of poverty' which is viewed by some as a way of life in itself rather than as a form of adaptation in order to survive. The environmental characteristics of the adopted and illegitimate children as a group to some extent echo these stereotypes, but closer examination shows that there are important differences. To what extent are they due to birth status?

The very favourable circumstances in which the adopted children were living at the age of 11 were not wholly related to social class, as adopted children in working-class families were also likely to be living in financially secure homes with good access to space and amenities. Stringent selection procedures were likely to have made high material standards a requirement at the time of adoption, but they do not necessarily explain their continuation (and improvement) over an 11-year period. It has been suggested (see Chapter 16) that these favourable circumstances at 11 were in part likely to be due to the significantly smaller family size of the adoptive families, which, in turn, made it easier to attain or maintain high material standards.

Although small family size may have been a distinctive feature of adoptive status in the past, it is no more a prerogative than marriage or togetherness is to legitimate status. The 1970 birth cohort (Chamberlain *et al.*, 1975) is, for example, likely to show considerable differences from the 1958 cohort in the pattern of family size, owing to changes in the birthrate and the effects of the Abortion Act 1967. In recent years, too, there has been a considerable change in the pattern of adoption placements as fewer babies have become available and as the needs of older or handicapped children or those with brothers and sisters have been realised (Rowe and Lambert, 1973). Adoption agencies are now more ready to consider placing children in families where there are perhaps several other children, or else creating a medium- or even large-sized family by placing several children together. Material standards have probably, in turn, become a less important feature of selection (though a basic ability to cope is still likely to be required) and the possibility of financial subsidies to adopters has been provided for in the Children Act 1975. Future studies of adopted children would seem unlikely to find the very high material standards which the children in this 1958 cohort enjoyed, and these standards will probably be seen to relate to a particular era in adoption rather than being a special feature of adoptive status.

This is especially likely to be so if there continues to be a failure to ensure adequate living standards for all children, as measured by, for example, income, space or amenities, which is highlighted by the situation of the illegitimate children as a group and by both illegitimate and legitimate children living in certain parental situations. Many of the poorer circumstances of the illegitimate children, as a group, would seem to be related to their working-class background and to a tendency towards downward rather than upward social mobility. The results of lower earning ability are reflected in the higher proportions claiming state benefits, and, to some extent, in the lack of household amenities and in overcrowding.

Family size plays a complex part in this picture, as the families in which illegitimate children were living were often smaller than those of legitimate children, but there was also a higher proportion of illegitimate children in large families. When this was related to family situation, though, only the illegitimate children living with both their natural parents showed a tendency to live in large families more often than their legitimate counterparts. The illegitimate children living with both natural parents tended to be at a disadvantage also as far as income and housing were concerned, and family size cannot have been the sole explanation for this. It has been suggested (see Chapter 16) that a greater ambiguity in their parents' marital status may have placed some of those parents in a weaker position for obtaining, say, reasonable housing. Whether this is so or not, this group illustrates the cumulative disadvantages that poverty can bring, and these have little relevance to birth status as such. Very many other illegitimate children, including ones living with both natural parents, were living in adequate housing and were not dependent on state benefits.

There were no significant differences in the circumstances of legitimate or illegitimate children living in step-families, and those among children in one-parent families could be linked with the presence or absence of a matrimonial home. Children in these situations were less well provided for in material terms than legitimate children living with both natural parents. This suggests that, whatever the children's birth status, their parents experienced greater difficulty in acquiring or keeping such things as a reasonable income or reasonable housing, particularly if they were lone parents. The difficulties faced by these parents have been highlighted by the Finer report (DHSS, 1974) and many other studies. Recent changes in allowances for children, a higher earnings threshold for supplementary benefits, and attempts to lessen housing discrimination have followed since 1974, but there is still a reluctance to tackle the underlying problems of poverty.

Developmental outcomes

The association of environmental factors with children's development is very well known (Davie *et al.*, 1972; Douglas *et al.*, 1968; Rutter *et al.*, 1970; Clarke and Clarke, 1974). For this reason we took into account both the family situation and environmental factors when looking at the relationship between birth status and the children's development at 11. The results showed that it was necessary to do this if erroneous impressions were not to be formed.

The procedure of allowing for background characteristics does not hide the fact that when faced by a public examination, for example, children in one group may do markedly better than the other groups. It seeks to answer the question whether this prowess is due to birth status or whether children living in similar environmental circumstances, legitimate or illegitimate, are likely to achieve similar results.

When no allowance was made for background circumstances, adopted children were, for example, reading better at 11, on average, than either legitimate children or illegitimate children. This achievement deserves to be commended, but when we looked at the reading scores of children who came from homes with similar environmental characteristics, illegitimate as well as legitimate children were reading just as well as the adopted. Conversely, where the home circumstances were less favourable, illegitimate children were not reading any worse than other children in such circumstances. The fact that illegitimate children were more likely than other children to be living in disadvantaged situations, rather than their birth status, was associated with their lower reading scores at 11. For most of the children the same was also true when maths ability was considered. The findings also showed that at the age of 11 children's physical growth was unlikely to be related to birth status.

When the children's social adjustment at 11 was considered within the context of their background circumstances, there continued to be a difference between illegitimate and legitimate children, and the apparently equivocal position of the adopted children tilted in the direction of the illegitimate. Although the adjustment of these two groups appeared similar, varying stress factors may have been at work in each group, even if, ultimately, they were all linked with birth status.

At the age of 7 the adopted children had already been showing signs of having more behaviour problems than legitimate children

(Seglow *et al.*, 1972). Between the ages of 7 and 11 all children are likely to have had periods of doubt and uncertainty about their origins and identity, and all but a handful of the adopted children knew for a fact that they were born to a different parents but probably did not know a great deal about them. By 1969, when these children were 11, the policy of greater openness in talking to adopted children about their origins was increasingly encouraged by professionals and the media. But, with the best will in the world, it is not an easy matter to put into practice, and may have added to, rather than diminished, the children's difficulties in adjustment. The finding, in other studies of adopted children, that there was an increase in problems around this age, followed by a later settling down, suggests that it may be a healthy sign that the adopted children in the NCDS were more troublesome in mid-childhood. It will be extremely interesting to study their adjustment at 16 to see what was happening during adolescence. Obviously teachers and parents would be right to show concern for difficulties in social adjustment at any age, but it may be the case that these are only an indication of possible maladjustment if they persist.

Illegitimate children who were not adopted were also more likely than legitimate children to have experienced difficulties in resolving uncertainties about their origins. Their mothers may have been more reluctant than adoptive parents to discuss the subject, and while some of the children were living with their own fathers, others may have been told even less about them than adopted children. However, the illegitimate children had been less well adjusted than legitimate children at the age of 7, which suggests that unless uncertainty about their origins was the contributory reason at both ages, other factors, such as the greater amount of change in their environmental circumstances, were also associated with their relatively poorer social adjustment at 11.

In conclusion

The general lack of association between children's physical development or their school attainment at the age of 11 and their birth status is a salutory reminder of the powerful influence of the environment for good or ill. Some children were fortunate and lived in an exceptionally favourable environment, and many of the adopted children were among this group. For other children, living in families with poor housing and low income, and experiencing the difficulties mainly associated with low social status were far more pressing and ever-present problems than whether their parents had been married when they were born.

Even if they were legitimately born, diversity in family life was becoming the experience of an increasing proportion of children, as their parents' marriages were broken or remade. The importance of birth status fades before a recognition of the practical needs of families for such things as adequate incomes and adequate housing if children are to grow up without disadvantage.

Illegitimacy and adoption are fascinating subjects, which deserve attention. Singling out such children and comparing them with legitimate children, in the way that has been done in this report, highlights their differences less than the needs shared by all children in changing families.

Appendix 1

Note on Statistical Analysis

by Jenny Head

In all tables where tests of significance have been carried out the level of significance is indicated as follows:

		P	<	0.001	***
0.001	<	P	<	0.01	**
0.01	<	P	<	0.05	*
Otherwise		P	>	0.05	

Contingency tables

In most cases a test for independence in the table has been carried out by means of Pearson's χ^2 test. Where appropriate, a test for a linear trend has been used. In this case it is desired to test whether the proportion (Pi) has a linear trend over the k levels (ti) of the other factor of interest. This model may be written

$$Pi = \alpha + \beta t_i$$

and the method of analysis is described in Bhapkar (1968).

There were three comparisons that might be made in any table, as follows:

(i) between illegitimate and legitimate children;
(ii) between adopted and legitimate children;
(iii) between illegitimate and adopted children.

The degrees of freedom (df) used in tests (with the exception described below) take into account the possible multiple comparisons for any table, although in some cases, after examining the data, it was decided not to test all three differences. Thus for a table of legitimacy status by a k-level factor, the degrees of freedom for, for example, the comparison between illegitimate and legitimate will be $2(k-1)$. See Gabriel (1966) for a description of this technique. However, where differences have been looked at within family situation, it was known *a priori* that comparisons would only be made between illegitimate and legitimate, and so the degrees of freedom for these tests were $(k - 1)$.

Analysis of variance

Where the variable of interest was measured on an interval scale, such as test scores, analysis of variance was used. This technique estimates differences in mean scores on the dependent variable between the levels of one factor after adjusting for all other factors in the analysis. The main model used is one in which the effects of the different factors are assumed to be additive. Fitted constants are presented for each factor and these sum to zero over the levels of each factor. The difference between the fitted constants is given for those factors with only two levels.

Tests of significance for the different factors have been done by means of chi-square rather than F values, because the large sample sizes mean that these are practically equivalent.

In some cases where it was suspected that the additivity assumption may not hold, interactions were tested. A first order interaction will estimate differences in mean scores between the levels of one independent variable for each level of another independent variable.

The distributions of all the dependent variables have been examined, and an appropriate variance stabilising transformation was used for the Bristol Social Adjustment Guide $(Y = sq. \ rt \ (x + 0.375))$. The raw scores of the other variables were approximately normally distributed and the variances were sufficiently stable.

In the analysis of variance with legitimacy status as an independent variable, it was desired to make all three comparisons between each pair of status groups, and thus a multiple comparison test devised by Scheffé (1959) was used. In the analyses of variance with family situation and legitimacy status as one of the independent variables, it was decided *a priori* that the contrasts of interest were those between the group with two natural parents at 7 and 11 and each of the other four groups. Thus one degree of freedom was used for each of these contrasts, which were only examined if the overall test was significant.

Analysis of covariance was used to examine the change in social adjustment, reading and maths scores between 7 and 11 for the three legitimacy status groups. This estimates the mean scores at 11 for the levels of each factor for a given 7-year score. Thus the fitted constants for legitimacy status in this analysis tell us what the differences in mean scores at 11 for the three groups would be, on average, for any given score at 7. The relationship between the 11- and 7-year scores was examined and found to be approximately linear for the maths and social adjustment, but for reading the relationship was non-linear for high 7-year scores. Therefore, the scale of the 7-year reading scores was transformed to give an approximately linear relationship (Fogelman and Goldstein, 1976).

The analysis of change between 7 and 11 was also carried out, making adjustments for possible measurement errors in the 7-year score. Values of 0.9 and 0.8 for the reliabilities of the 7-year score chosen, and the variances of the

7-year scores, were adjusted for the possible measurement error, using these values (Warren *et al.*, 1974). This adjustment for possible measurement error made little difference to the results (see Table A13.3).

Appendix 2

Tables

			N
Identified at birth (3–9 March 1958)			669
Unavoidable losses:	stillborn	21	
	neonatal deaths	18	
		39	
Surviving four weeks after birth			630
Gains: Illegitimate births identified during			
follow-up at seven years		10	640
Unavoidable losses:	died	11	
	emigrated	11	
Avoidable losses:	refused	4	
	untraced	66	
		92	
	(errors	5)	
Adopted by 7-year follow-up			180†
Sample of illegitimate/not adopted at 7			363†
Sample of illegitimate at 11			543
Unavoidable losses:	died	1	
	emigrated	16	
Avoidable losses:	refused	39	
	untraced/no parental	78	
		134	
Adopted by 7, with data at 11			115
Illegitimate/not adopted by 7 with data at 11			294

† These numbers differ from those given in *Born Illegitimate* (Crellin *et al.*, 1971, p. 57 and Table A8.1), as, since the time of the 7-year follow-up, errors have been corrected in the light of earlier information.

TABLE A7.1 *Patterns of change in family situation between 7 and 11 – see also Table 7.2*

Change between 7 and 11 to living with	Illegitimate		Legitimate	
	N	%	N	%
Both natural parents	5	12.2	20	3.4
Step/adoptive parents	13	31.7	172	29.1
Lone parent (from 2 parents)	13 ⎫	31.7 ⎫	297 ⎫	50.2 ⎫
Lone parent (from other sit.)	8 ⎭ 21	19.5 ⎭ 51.2	24 ⎭ 321	4.1 ⎭ 54.3
Other situations	2	4.9	78	13.2
Total	41	100	591	100

TABLE A7.2   *Family situation at 11 by legitimacy status and social class*

(a) Non-manual

Legitimacy status	Natural parents	Step-parents	Adoptive parents	Mother alone	Father alone	Other sits	Total
Illegitimate	19 (58%)	10 (30%)	–	–	1 (3%)	3 (9%)	33 (100%)
Adopted	–	–	61 (94%)	–	–	4 (6%)	65 (100%)
Legitimate	3 874 (97%)	80 (2%)	1 –	–	20 –	28 (1%)	4 003 (100%)

(b) Manual

Legitimacy status	Natural parents	Step-parents	Adoptive parents	Mother alone	Father alone	Other sits	Total
Illegitimate	99 (54%)	61 (33%)	0 (–)	0 (–)	1 (1%)	22 (12%)	183 (100%)
Adopted	0	0	42 (95%)	0	0	2 (5%)	44 (100%)
Legitimate	6 982 (95%)	224 (3%)	2 (–)	0 (–)	63 (1%)	96 (1%)	7 367 (100%)

(c) No male head

Legitimacy status	Natural parents	Step-parents	Adoptive parents	Mother alone	Father alone	Other sits	Total
Illegitimate	0	0	0	58 (84%)	0	11 (16%)	69 (100%)
Adopted	0	0	0	0	0	0	0 (–)
Legitimate	0	0	0	502 (94%)	0	33 (6%)	535 (100%)

Illegitimate: natural parents/all other family situations by non-manual/manual χ^2(1df) = 0.03
Legitimate: natural parents/all other family situations by non-manual/manual χ^2(1df) = 23.7***
No male head: mother alone/other by legit/illeg χ^2(1df) = 7.3**

TABLE A7.3 *Children in care by family situation at 11*

Family situation		Long stay before 7	Short stay before 7	Between 7–11	Other answers	Never in care	Total	Not known
Natural parents	Illeg	2 (2%)	6 (5%)	2 (2%)	1 (1%)	102 (90%)	113 (100%)	9
	Legit	25 (–)	83 (1%)	80 (1%)	32 (–)	10 304 (98%)	10 524 (100%)	482
Step-parents	Illeg	2 (3%)	1 (1%)	4 (6%)	0 (–)	62 (90%)	69 (100%)	3
	Legit	6 (2%)	17 (6%)	4 (1%)	4 (1%)	252 (89%)	283 (100%)	22
Mother alone	Illeg	2 (4%)	7 (15%)	3 (6%)	0 (–)	35 (74%)	47 (100%)	11
	Legit	4 (1%)	15 (3%)	17 (4%)	5 (1%)	421 (91%)	462 (100%)	41
Father alone	Illeg	0 (–)	1 (50%)	0 (–)	0 (–)	1 (50%)	2 (100%)	0
	Legit	3 (4%)	3 (4%)	3 (4%)	1 (1%)	70 (87%)	80 (100%)	4
Other situations	Illeg	9 (24%)	1 (3%)	1 (3%)	2 (5%)	25 (66%)	38 (100%)	2
	Legit	25 (16%)	6 (4%)	18 (11%)	4 (2%)	107 (67%)	160 (100%)	10

Natural parents: Illeg/legit by in care/never χ^2(1df) = 30.8***
Step-parents: Illeg/legit by in care/never χ^2(1df) = 0.0
Mother alone: Illeg/legit by in care/never χ^2(1df) = 15.2***

TABLE A8.1   *Social class of origin and at 11*

Social class of origin	Social class at 11			
	Non-manual	*Manual*	*No male head (NMH)*	*Total*
(a) Illegitimate				
Non-manual (NM)	12 (23%)	33 (62%)	8 (15%)	53 (100%)
Manual (M)	13 (8%)	118 (69%)	40 (23%)	171 (100%)
Not classified/NK	8 (13%)	32 (53%)	21 (34%)	61 (100%)
Total	33 (12%)	183 (64%)	69 (24%)	285 (100%)
(b) Adopted				
Non-manual	18 (78%)	5 (22%)		23 (100%)
Manual	34 (52%)	32 (48%)		66 (100%)
Not classified/NK	13 (65%)	7 (35%)		20 (100%)
Total	65 (60%)	44 (40%)		109 (100%)
(c) Legitimate				
Non-manual	1 404 (57%)	973 (39%)	92 (4%)	2 469 (100%)
Manual	2 012 (27%)	5 053 (68%)	336 (5%)	7 401 (100%)
Not classified/NK	590 (29%)	1 347 (66%)	108 (5%)	2 045 (100%)
Total	4 006 (34%)	7 373 (62%)	536 (4%)	11 915 (100%)

NM at origin: Illeg/legit by 11-year NM/M/NMH χ^2(4df) = 34.5***
M at origin: Illeg/legit by 11-year NM/M/NMH χ^2(4df) = 143.6***

Illegitimate: Origin (NM/M) by 11-year (NM/M/NMH) χ^2(2df) = 9.8**
Adopted: Origin (NM/M) by 11-year (NM/M) χ^2(1df) = 4.0*
Legitimate: Origin (NM/M) by 11-year (NM/M/NMH) χ^2(2df) = 726.7***

TABLE A8.2 *Sex distribution by social class at 11*

(a) Illegitimate

	Sex		
Social class	Boy	Girl	Total
Non-manual (NM)	15 (45%)	18 (55%)	33 (100%)
Manual (M)	73 (40%)	110 (60%)	183 (100%)
No male head (NMH)	30 (43%)	39 (57%)	69 (100%)

NM/M/NMH by boy/girl χ^2 (2df) = 0.5

(b) Adopted

	Sex		
Social class†	Boy	Girl	Total
Non-manual	35 (54%)	30 (46%)	65 (100%)
Manual	28 (64%)	16 (36%)	44 (100%)

† There were no adopted children without a male head of household
NM/M by boy/girl χ^2 (1df) = 0.7

(c) Legitimate

	Sex		
Social class	Boy	Girl	Total
Non-manual	2018 (50%)	1988 (50%)	4006 (100%)
Manual	3815 (52%)	3558 (48%)	7373 (100%)
No male head	258 (48%)	278 (52%)	536 (100%)

NM/M/NMH by boy/girl χ^2 (2df) = 3.9

TABLE A8.3 *Sex and family situation at 11*

Family situation		Boy	Girl	Total
Natural parents	Illegitimate	48 (39%)	74 (61%)	122 (100%)
	Legitimate†	5656 (51%)	5350 (49%)	11006 (100%)
Step-parents	Illegitimate	29 (40%)	43 (60%)	72 (100%)
	Legitimate	157 (51%)	148 (49%)	305 (100%)
Mother alone	Illegitimate	25 (43%)	33 (57%)	58 (100%)
	Legitimate	243 (48%)	260 (52%)	503 (100%)
Father alone	Illegitimate	2 (100%)	0 (–)	2 (100%)
	Legitimate	46 (55%)	38 (45%)	84 (100%)
Other situations	Illegitimate	20 (50%)	20 (50%)	40 (100%)
	Legitimate	85 (50%)	85 (50%)	170 (100%)
Adoptive parents		63 (59%)	44 (41%)	107 (100%)

† Numbers for this group vary slightly from Table 7.1, owing to further updating of tapes.

Natural parents: Illeg/legit by sex $\chi^2(1df) = 6.5*$
Step-parents: Illeg/legit by sex $\chi^2(1df) = 2.5$
Mother alone: Illeg/legit by sex $\chi^2(1df) = 0.4$

TABLE A8.4   *Family size by legitimacy status and social class at 11*

(a) Non-manual

Legitimacy status	Number of children in family						
	1	2	1–2 (small)	3–4 (medium)	5+ (large)	Total	NK
Illegitimate	6	13	19 (58%)	6 (18%)	8 (24%)	33 (100%)	0
Adopted	17	36	53 (83%)	11 (17%)	0 (–)	64 (100%)	1
Legitimate	443	1 571	2 014 (50%)	1 659 (42%)	322 (8%)	3 995 (100%)	11

(b) Manual

Legitimacy status	Number of children in family						
	1	2	1–2 (small)	3–4 (medium)	5+ (large)	Total	NK
Illegitimate	20	40	60 (33%)	84 (46%)	39 (21%)	183 (100%)	0
Adopted	17	16	33 (75%)	9 (20%)	2 (5%)	44 (100%)	0
Legitimate	730	2 245	2 975 (40%)	2 993 (41%)	1 382 (19%)	7 350 (100%)	23

TABLE A8.4—continued
(c) **No male head**

Legitimacy status†	Number of children in family						
	1	2	1–2 (small)	3–4 (medium)	5+ (large)	Total	NK
Illegitimate	27	13	40 (65%)	12 (20%)	9 (15%)	61 (100%)	8
Legitimate	89	161	250 (48%)	194 (37%)	81 (15%)	525 (100%)	11

† There were no adopted children in this category.

Non-manual: Illeg/legit by family size (1–2; 3–4; 5+) χ^2(4df) = 15.1**
 Adop/legit by family size (1–2; 3+) χ^2(2df) = 25.2***
 Illeg/adop by family size (1–2; 3+) χ^2(2df) = 6.0*

Manual: Illeg/legit by family size (1–2; 3–4; 5+) χ^2(4df) = 4.4
 Adop/legit by family size (1–2; 3+) χ^2(2df) = 20.2***
 Illeg/adop by family size (1–2; 3+) χ^2(2df) = 24.4***

No male head: Illeg/legit by family size (1–2; 3–4; 5+) χ^2(2df) = 8.2*
Adopted: Non-manual/manual by family size (1–2; 3+) χ^2(1df) = 0.6

TABLE A10.1 *Crowding at 7 and 11* (more than 1.5 persons per room)
(a) **Illegitimate (N = 242 = 100%)**

	Overcrowded at 11	Not overcrowded at 11
Overcrowded at 7	27 (11%)	23 (9%)
Not overcrowded at 7	16 (7%)	176 (73%)

(b) **Adopted (N = 90 = 100%)**

	Overcrowded at 11	Not overcrowded at 11
Overcrowded at 7	2 (2%)	4 (5%)
Not overcrowded at 7	1 (1%)	83 (92%)

(c) **Legitimate (N = 11 185 = 100%)**

	Overcrowded at 11	Not overcrowded at 11
Overcrowded at 7	883 (8%)	700 (6%)
Not overcrowded at 7	374 (3%)	9 228 (83%)

Illeg/legit by crowded 7 and 11 (both 7 and 11; 7, not 11; not 7; not 7 or 11)
χ^2 (6df) = 17.3**
Illeg/legit by crowded 7 and 11 (crowded 7 or 11; not 7 or 11) χ^2 (6df) = 14.9*
Illeg/legit by crowded 7 and 11 (crowded 7 and 11; other groups)
χ^2 (6df) = 3.0
Adop/legit by crowded 7 and 11 (crowded 7 or 11; not crowded 7 and 11)
χ^2 (2df) = 5.2

TABLE A10.2   *Crowding at 11 by family situation*

Family situation		Crowding at 11					
		≤ 1.0	> 1.0	> 1.5	> 2.0	Total	NA
Natural parents	Illeg	48 (39%)	44 (36%)	25 (20%)	5 (4%)	122 (100%)	0
	Legit	6675 (61%)	3026 (27%)	1017 (9%)	269 (2%)	10987 (100%)	17
Step-parents	Illeg	32 (44%)	30 (42%)	9 (13%)	1 (1%)	72 (100%)	0
	Legit	151 (49%)	106 (35%)	36 (12%)	12 (4%)	305 (100%)	1
Mother alone	Illeg	31 (60%)	15 (29%)	5 (10%)	1 (2%)	52 (100%)	6
	Legit	348 (70%)	106 (21%)	37 (7%)	4 (1%)	495 (100%)	9
Father alone	Illeg	2 (100%)	0 (–)	0 (–)	0 (–)	2 (100%)	0
	Legit	71 (84%)	7 (8%)	5 (6%)	1 (1%)	84 (100%)	0
Other sits	Illeg	27 (71%)	9 (24%)	2 (5%)	0 (–)	38 (100%)	2
	Legit	95 (62%)	44 (29%)	9 (6%)	4 (3%)	152 (100%)	16
Adoptive parents		95 (90%)	8 (7%)	3 (3%)	0 (–)	106 (100%)	1

Mother alone: Illeg/legit by crowding at 11 (< 1.0, > 1.5, > 2.0)
χ^2_2 (trend) = 2.0 (1df)
χ^2 (departure from trend) = 0.2 (1df)
Natural parents: Illeg/legit by crowding at 11 (< 1.0, > 1.5, > 2.0)
χ^2_2 (trend) = 20.6 (1df)***
χ^2 (departure from trend) = 0.0 (1df)
Illegitimate: Natural parents/step-parents by crowding at 11 (< 1.0, > 1.5, > 2.0)
χ^2_2 (trend) = 2.5 (1df)
χ^2 (departure from trend) = 1.2 (1df)
Legitimate: Natural parents/step-parents by crowding at 11 (< 1.0, > 1.5, > 2.0)
χ^2_2 (trend) = 13.2 (1df)***
χ^2 (departure from trend) = 1.3 (1df)

TABLE A10.3 *Amenities at 7 and 11 (use of indoor lavatory, bathroom and hot-water supply)*

(a) Illegitimate (N = 254 = 100 %)

	At 11		
At 7	Sole use all 3	Shared use 2/1	Shared all/no use
Sole use all 3	145 (57%)	10 (4%)	5 (2%)
Shared use 2/1	22 (9%)	17 (7%)	2 (1%)
Shared all/no use	19 (7%)	15 (6%)	19 (7%)

(b) Adopted (N = 95 = 100 %)

	At 11		
At 7	Sole use all 3	Shared use 2/1	Shared all/no use
Sole use all 3	89 (94%)	1 (1%)	0 (–)
Shared use 2/1	4 (4%)	1 (1%)	0 (–)
Shared all/no use	0 (–)	0 (–)	0 (–)

(c) Legitimate (N = 11 364 = 100 %)

	At 11		
At 7	Sole use all 3	Shared use 2/1	Shared all/no use
Sole use all 3	9 062 (80%)	277 (2%)	64 (1%)
Shared use 2/1	658 (6%)	606 (5%)	47 (–)
Shared all/no use	356 (3%)	120 (1%)	174 (2%)

Illeg/legit by amenities (sole all 7 + 11; shared 7 sole all 11; sole all 7 shared 11; shared 7 and 11) χ^2 (6df) = 82.4***
Adop/legit by amenities (sole all 7 + 11; shared 7 or 11) χ^2 (2df) = 11.4**

TABLE A10.4   *Amenities at 11 by family situation*

Family situation at 11		Sole use all 3	Shared use 2/1	Shared all/ no use	Total	NA
Natural parents	Illeg	88 (73%)	17 (14%)	16 (13%)	121 (100%)	1
	Legit	9 685 (89%)	940 (9%)	246 (2%)	10 871 (100%)	133
Step-parents	Illeg	54 (77%)	13 (19%)	3 (4%)	70 (100%)	2
	Legit	256 (85%)	32 (11%)	11 (4%)	299 (100%)	7
Mother alone	Illeg	33 (63%)	12 (23%)	7 (13%)	52 (100%)	6
	Legit	381 (78%)	66 (14%)	39 (8%)	486 (100%)	18
Father alone	Illeg	2 (100%)	0 (–)	0 (–)	2 (100%)	0
	Legit	67 (81%)	9 (11%)	7 (8%)	83 (100%)	1
Other situations	Illeg	33 (87%)	3 (8%)	2 (5%)	38 (100%)	2
	Legit	129 (85%)	14 (9%)	8 (5%)	151 (100%)	17
Adoptive parents		103 (97%)	3 (3%)	0 (–)	106 (100%)	1

Natural parents: Illeg/legit by amenities (sole all/shared 2, 1/shared all)
  χ^2 (trend) = 12.1** (1df)
  χ^2 (departure from trend) = 4.1* (1df)
Step-parents: Illeg/legit by amenities (sole all/shared 2, 1/shared all)
  χ^2 (trend) = 1.5 (1df)
  χ^2 (departure from trend) = 1.2 (1df)
Mother alone: Illeg/legit by amenities (sole all/shared 2, 1/shared all)
  χ^2 (trend) = 3.8* (1df)
  χ^2 (departure from trend) = 0.6 (1df)

TABLE A10.5   *Tenure and family situation at 11*

Family situation		Tenure at 11					Other/NA
		Owned	Council	Private	Tied	Total	
Natural parents	Illeg	39 (32%)	64 (53%)	14 (12%)	4 (3%)	121 (100%)	1
	Legit	5 195 (47%)	4 567 (42%)	715 (7%)	495 (4%)	10 972 (100%)	32
Step-parents	Illeg	21 (29%)	39 (54%)	10 (14%)	2 (3%)	72 (100%)	0
	Legit	124 (41%)	134 (44%)	36 (12%)	8 (3%)	302 (100%)	4
Mother alone	Illeg	6 (12%)	32 (62%)	12 (23%)	2 (4%)	52 (100%)	6
	Legit	132 (27%)	282 (57%)	68 (14%)	9 (2%)	491 (100%)	13
Father alone	Illeg	1 (50%)	1 (50%)	0 (−)	0 (−)	2 (100%)	0
	Legit	30 (36%)	43 (51%)	7 (8%)	4 (5%)	84 (100%)	0
Other sits	Illeg	8 (21%)	23 (61%)	4 (11%)	3 (8%)	38 (100%)	2
	Legit	40 (26%)	91 (59%)	15 (10%)	7 (5%)	153 (100%)	15
Adoptive parents		70 (66%)	27 (25%)	5 (5%)	4 (4%)	106 (100%)	1

Natural parents: Illeg/legit by owned/other χ^2 (1df) = 10.4**
Step-parents: Illeg/legit by owned/other χ^2 (1df) = 3.0
Mother alone: Illeg/legit by owned/other χ^2 (1df) = 5.1*

TABLE A10.6   *Tenure at 7 and 11*

Tenure at 7	Tenure at 11				
	Owned	Council rented	Privately rented	Tied/rent-free	Total
(a) Owned					
Illegitimate	58 (87%)	8 (12%)	1 (1%)	0 (–)	67 (100%)
Adopted	61 (97%)	1 (2%)	1 (2%)	0 (–)	63 (100%)
Legitimate	4 647 (95%)	142 (3%)	75 (2%)	52 (1%)	4 916 (100%)
(b) Council rented					
Illegitimate	1 (1%)	113 (94%)	6 (5%)	0 (–)	120 (100%)
Adopted	4 (13%)	27 (87%)	0 (–)	0 (–)	31 (100%)
Legitimate	303 (6%)	4 267 (91%)	70 (2%)	58 (1%)	4 698 (100%)
(c) Privately rented					
Illegitimate	6 (11%)	20 (36%)	27 (48%)	3 (5%)	56 (100%)
Adopted	1 (25%)	0 (–)	2 (50%)	1 (25%)	4 (100%)
Legitimate	264 (20%)	354 (27%)	615 (46%)	99 (7%)	1 332 (100%)
(d) Rent-free					
Illegitimate	2 (20%)	3 (30%)	0 (–)	5 (50%)	10 (100%)
Adopted	0 (–)	0 (–)	0 (–)	0 (–)	0 (–)
Legitimate	51 (20%)	36 (14%)	14 (5%)	158 (61%)	259 (100%)

Owned at 7: Illeg/legit by owned/other at 11 χ^2(2df) = 9.1*
Owned at 7: Adop/legit by owned/other at 11 χ^2(2df) = 0.3
Council rented at 7: Illeg/legit by council rent/other at 11 χ^2(2df) = 1.2
Council rented at 7: Adop/legit by council rent/other at 11 χ^2(2df) = 0.9
Private rented at 7: Illeg/legit by owned/council rent/priv. rent at 11 χ^2(2df) = 3.9*

TABLE A12.1 *Height at 11 and legitimacy status (AOV)*

Independent variables	Dependent variable = Height at 11 (cm)			
	F Constant	SE	DF	χ^2
Overall constant	80.2			
Mother's height (cm)	0.39		1	1 179.0***
Legitimacy status				
Illegitimate	−0.5		2	1.3
Adopted	0.5			
Legitimate	0.0			
Sex: Male/female	−0.9		1	41.8***
Social class				
Origin 11				
NM NM	0.6		5	58.9***
M M	−0.8			
NM M	0.0			
M NM	0.0			
NM NMH	1.3			
M NMH	−1.1			
Number of children				
1–2	1.2		2	110.0***
3–4	−0.2			
5+	−1.0			
Free school meals/not	−1.1		1	16.6***
Crowding: ⩽ 1.5–> 1.5	1.6		1	28.4***
Amenities				
Sole use 3	−0.0		3	3.3
Sole use 2	−0.5			
Sole use 1	0.4			
Sole use 0	0.1			
Interactions				
Legitimacy status by sex			2	3.9
Sex by social class			5	6.1
Legitimacy status by no. of children			4	2.8
Legitimacy status by crowding			2	2.4
Legitimacy status by social class†			8	5.0
(a) Fitting all main effects				
Illeg–legit	−0.5	0.5	2	0.8
Adop–legit	0.5	0.7	2	0.5
Illeg–adop	−1.0	0.9	2	1.2

continued overleaf

TABLE A12.1–continued

Independent variables	Dependent variable = Height at 11 (cm)			
	F Constant	SE	DF	χ^2
Sample size		8 789		
Total variance		53.34		
Residual mean square		44.09		
Dependent variable mean		144.5		
Fitting legitimacy status alone		(N)		
Overall constant	144.7			
Illegitimate	−1.3	(183)	2	8.1*
Adopted	1.4	(82)		
Legitimate	−0.1	(8524)		
(*b*) *Fitting legitimacy status alone*				
Illeg–legit	−1.2	0.5.	2	4.2
Adop–legit	1.5	0.8	2	3.8
Illeg–adop	−2.7	1.0	2	7.8*

† There are 8 df for this interaction, as there were no adopted children in either of the last two categories of the social class variable.

The abbreviations M (manual), NM (non-manual) and NMH (no male head) are used in this and several of the remaining tables.

TABLE A12.2 *Height at 11 and family situation (AOV)*

Independent variables	F Constant	SE	DF	χ^2
	Dependent variable = Height at 11 (cm)			
Overall constant	80.3			
Mother's height (cm)	0.39	0.01	1	1 056.0***
Family situation and legitimacy status			4	4.3
(a) Legit 2NP 7 and 11	0.0			
(b) Legit step 7 and 11	0.4			
(c) Adopted 7 and 11	0.4			
(d) Illeg 2NP 7 and 11	0.9			
(e) Illeg step 7 and 11	-1.7			
Sex: Boy–Girl	-0.8	0.01	1	32.5***
Social class Origin 11			3	48.5***
NM NM	0.6			
M M	-0.8			
NM M	0.1			
M NM	0.1			
Number of children			2	92.3***
1–2	1.2			
3–4	-0.2			
5+	-1.0			
Free school meals/not	-1.3	0.3	1	17.2***
Crowding: ≤1.5–>1.5	1.4	0.3	1	22.0***
Amenities			3	5.0
Sole use 3	-0.1			
Sole use 2	-0.6			
Sole use 1	0.5			
Sole use 0	0.2			
Interaction Family situation and legitimacy status by sex			4	3.7
Sample size	7 882			
Total variance	52.9			
Residual mean square	43.9			
Dependent variable mean	144.6			

continued overleaf

TABLE A12.2–continued

Independent variables	Dependent variable = Height at 11 (cm)			
	F Constant	SE	DF	χ^2
Fit family situation and legitimacy status alone		(N)		
Overall constant	144.3			
(a) Legit 2NP 7 and 11	0.3	(7 632)	4	8.0
(b) Legit step 7 and 11	0.0	(75)		
(c) Adopted 7 and 11	1.6	(76)		
(d) Illeg 2NP 7 and 11	0.3	(67)		
(e) Illeg step 7 and 11	−2.2	(41)		

The abbreviation NP (natural parent) is used in this and several of the remaining tables.

TABLE A13.1   (i) *Reading at 11* (ii) *Maths at 11 and legitimacy status (AOV)*

Independent variables	(i) Dependent variable = Reading score at 11 in years				(ii) Dependent variable = Maths score at 11 in years			
	F Constant	SE	DF	χ^2	F Constant	SE	DF	χ^2
Overall constant	10.2				10.2			
Legitimacy status								
Illegitimate	−0.3		2	5.7	−0.3		2	18.1***
Adopted	0.2				−0.1			
Legitimate	0.1				0.4			
Sex:								
Male/female	0.0	0.1	1	0.03	0.1	0.04	1	3.9*
Social class								
Origin 11								
NM NM	1.2		5	831.5***	1.1		5	871.5***
M M	−0.9				−0.7			
NM M	−0.4				−0.2			
M NM	0.4				0.4			
NM NMH	0.4				0.0			
M NMH	−0.7				−0.6			
Number of children								
1–2	0.7		2	261.6***	0.4		2	115.9***
3–4	0.0				0.0			
5+	−0.7				−0.4			

continued overleaf

Table A13.1—continued

Independent variables	(i) Dependent variable = Reading score at 11 in years				(ii) Dependent variable = Maths score at 11 in years			
	F Constant	SE	DF	χ^2	F Constant	SE	DF	χ^2
Free school meals/not	−1.0	0.1	1	91.6***	−0.7	0.1	1	75.1***
Crowding: ≤ 1.5 –> 1.5	0.3	0.1	1	6.5*	0.2	0.1	1	3.3
Amenities								
Sole use 3	0.5		3	49.4***	0.4		3	52.7***
Sole use 2	0.1				0.0			
Sole use 1	−0.2				−0.1			
Sole use 0	−0.4				−0.3			
Interactions								
Legitimacy status by sex			2	3.1			2	7.3*
Sex by social class			5	4.1			5	1.5
Legitimacy status by no. of children			4	4.3			4	7.4
Legitimacy status by crowding			2	4.6			2	3.7
Legitimacy status by social class †			8	9.5			8	12.4

TABLE A13.1 – continued

Independent variables	(i) Dependent variable = Reading score at 11 in years				(ii) Dependent variable = Maths score at 11 in years			
	F Constant	SE	DF	χ^2	F Constant	SE	DF	χ^2
(a) Fitting all main effects								
Illeg–legit	−0.4	0.2	2	5.8	−0.7	0.2	2	15.9***
Adop–legit	0.1	0.3	2	0.0	−0.5	0.2	2	3.0
Illeg–adop	−0.5	0.3	2	1.9	−0.2	0.3	2	0.4
Sample size	9 244				9 241			
Total variance	8.1				5.3			
Residual mean square	6.6				4.4			
Dependent variable mean	11.0				11.0			
Fit legitimacy status alone		(N)				(N)		
Overall constant	11.1				10.9			
Illegitimate	−1.0	(199)	2	33.9***	−0.8	(199)	2	46.3***
Adopted	0.9	(80)			0.5	(80)		
Legitimate	0.1	(8 965)			0.3	(8 962)		

continued overleaf

TABLE A13.1-continued

Independent variables	(i) Dependent variable = Reading score at 11 in years				(ii) Dependent variable = Maths score at 11 in years			
	F Constant	SE	DF	χ^2	F Constant	SE	DF	χ^2
(b) *Fitting legitimacy status alone*								
Illeg–legit	-1.1	0.2	2	26.7***	-1.1	0.2	2	45.8***
Adop–legit	0.8	0.3	2	6.9*	0.2	0.2	2	0.5
Illeg–adopt	-2.0	0.4	2	25.3***	-1.3	0.3	2	18.2***

Fitted constants for interaction–legitimacy status by sex adjusted for other variables in the analysis

	Legitimacy status		
	Illeg	Adop	Legit
Boy	0.1	-0.5	0.3
Girl	-0.6	0.4	0.2

† There are 8df for this interaction (Legit. Status by Soc. Class) as there were no adopted children in either of the last two categories of the Soc. Class variable.

TABLE A13.2   (i) Reading at 11 (ii) Maths at 11 and family situation

Independent variables	(i) Dependent variable = Reading score at 11 in years				(ii) Dependent variable = Maths score at 11 in years			
	F Constant	SE	DF	χ^2	F Constant	SE	DF	χ^2
Overall constant	10.1				10.2			
Family situation and legitimacy status								
(a) Legit 2NP 7 and 11	0.3		4	9.2	0.4		4	20.0***
(b) Legit step 7 and 11	−0.2				0.0			
(c) Adopted 7 and 11	0.3				0.0			
(d) Illeg 2NP 7 and 11	−0.2				−0.4			
(e) Illeg step 7 and 11	−0.2				0.0			
Sex: Boy–Girl	0.0	0.1	1	0.3	0.1	0.05	1	6.5*
Social class								
Origin 11								
NM NM	1.1		3	752.1***	0.9		3	777.9***
M M	−1.0				−0.8			
NM M	−0.4				−0.4			
M NM	0.3				0.3			
Number of children								
1–2	0.7		2	235.4***	0.4		2	105.4***
3–4	0.0				0.0			
5+	−0.7				−0.4			
Free school meals/not	−0.9	0.1	1	53.7***	−0.7	0.1	1	46.1***
Crowding: ≤ 1.5 − > 1.5	0.2	0.1	1	4.3	0.1	0.1	1	2.6

continued overleaf

TABLE A13.2—continued

Independent variables	(i) Dependent variable = Reading score at 11 in years				(ii) Dependent variable = Maths score at 11 in years			
	F Constant	SE	DF	χ^2	F Constant	SE	DF	χ^2
Amenities								
Sole use 3	0.5		3	44.9***	0.4		3	45.1***
Sole use 2	0.1				0.0			
Sole use 1	−0.3				−0.2			
Sole use 0	−0.3				−0.2			
Interaction								
Family situation and legitimacy status by sex			4	8.0			4	11.6*
For family situation and legitimacy status								
(a) *vs each of* (b)–(e)								
(a)–(b)					0.4	0.2	1	2.9
(a)–(c)					0.4	0.2	1	2.7
Fitting all　(a)–(d)					0.8	0.2	1	12.2***
main effects　(a)–(e)					0.4	0.3		2.5
Sample size	8 235				8 232			
Total variance	8.0				5.2			
Residual mean square	6.6				4.4			
Dependent variable mean	11.2				11.2			

Independent variables	(i) Dependent variable = Reading score at 11 in years				(ii) Dependent variable = Maths score at 11 in years			
	F Constant	SE	DF	χ²	F Constant	SE	DF	χ²
Fit family situation and legitimacy status alone								
Overall constant	10.7	(N)			10.6	(N)		
(a) Legit 2NP 7 and 11	0.6	(7956)	4	39.8***	0.6	(7953)	4	45.6***
(b) Legit step 7 and 11	−0.4	(85)	4		−0.1	(85)		
(c) Adopted 7 and 11	1.3	(74)			0.7	(74)		
(d) Illeg 2NP 7 and 11	−0.8	(78)			−0.8	(78)		
(e) Illeg step 7 and 11	−0.7	(42)			−0.4	(42)		
For family situation and legitimacy status								
(a) vs each of (b)–(e) Fitting family situation and legitimacy status alone								
(a)–(b)	1.0	0.3	1	10.2**	0.7	0.5	1	8.1**
(a)–(c)	−0.7	0.3	1	5.2*	−0.1	0.3	1	0.3
(a)–(d)	1.4	0.3	1	16.6***	1.4	0.3	1	28.9***
(a)–(e)	1.3	0.4	1	8.0**	1.0	0.3	1	8.9**

Maths: Fitted constants for interaction – family situation and legitimacy status by sex

Sex	Legit 2NP 7 and 11	Legit step 7 and 11	Adopted 7 and 11	Illeg 2NP 7 and 11	Illeg step 7 and 11
Male	0.4	−0.1	−0.4	0.2	0.5
Female	0.3	0.0	0.6	−0.9	−0.6

TABLE A13.3   (i) *Changes in reading 7–11* (ii) *Changes in maths 7–11 and legitimacy status*

Independent variables	(i) Dependent variable = Reading score at 11 in years				(ii) Dependent variable = Maths score at 11 in years			
	F Constant	SE	DF	χ^2	F Constant	SE	DF	χ^2
Overall constant	6.1				7.8			
7-year score (measured about mean)	0.79	0.01	1	4 749.0***	0.61	0.01	1	3 620.0***
Legitimacy status								
Illegitimate	0.0		2	0.1	−0.1		2	9.1*
Adopted	0.0				−0.1			
Legitimate	0.0				0.2			
Sex: Boy–Girl	0.4	0.04	1	91.2***	0.0		1	1.0
Social class								
Origin 11								
NM NM	0.7		5	406.1***	0.8		5	574.5***
M M	−0.6				−0.5			
NM M	−0.2				−0.1			
M NM	0.2				0.3			
NM NMH	0.2				−0.1			
M NMH	−0.3				−0.4			
Number of children								
1–2	0.4		2	149.4***	0.3		2	122.7***
3–4	−0.1				0.0			
5+	−0.3				−0.3			
Free school meals/not	−0.4	0.1	1	20.2***	−0.4		1	34.7***
Crowding: ≤1.5− >1.5	0.3	0.1	1	10.0**	0.0		1	0.2

Independent variables	(i) Dependent variable = Reading score at 11 in years				(ii) Dependent variable = Maths score at 11 in years			
	F Constant	SE	DF	χ^2	F Constant	SE	DF	χ^2
Amenities								
Sole use 3	0.2		3	12.3**	0.3		3	54.0***
Sole use 2	0.0				0.0			
Sole use 1	−0.1				−0.2			
Sole use 0	−0.1				−0.1			
Interactions								
Legitimacy status by sex			2	5.2			2	8.0*
Legitimacy status by 7-year score			2	1.8			2	6.3*
Sample size	9 001				8 972			
Total variance		8.0				5.2		
Residual mean square		4.3				3.2		
Dependent variable mean		11.0				11.0		
Fit legitimacy status and 7-year score alone								
7-year score	0.85	0.01	1	6 012.0***	0.68	0.01	1	4 178.0***
Legitimacy status:								
Illegitimate	−0.3		2	5.7	−0.5		2	25.2***
Adopted	0.4				0.3			
Legitimate	−0.1				0.2			

continued overleaf

TABLE A13.3—continued

Independent variables	(i) Dependent variable = Reading score at 11 in years				(ii) Dependent variable = Maths score at 11 in years			
	F Constant	SE	DF	χ²	F Constant	SE	DF	χ²
Interaction: Legitimacy status by 7-year score			2	1.7			2	6.1*
Fit legitimacy status, 7-year score + other variables (as in full model above) *with reliability†* of 7-year score = 0.9(0.8)	Fitted constants				Fitted constants			
Legitimacy status								
Illegitimate	0.0 (0.0)				−0.1 (−0.1)			
Adopted	0.0 (0.0)				−0.1 (−0.1)			
Legitimate	0.0 (0.0)				0.2 (0.2)			

† See Appendix 1 for discussion on reliability of 7-year scores.

Maths–Fitted constants for interactions adjusted for other variables in the analysis

	Legit status by sex		
	Illeg	Adopted	Legit
Boy	0.2	−0.3	0.1
Girl	−0.4	0.2	0.2

	Legit status by 7-year maths score (measured about 7-year mean)	
	Intercept	Slope
Illeg	0.4	0.47
Adopted	−0.6	0.77
Legit	0.2	0.60

TABLE A14.1   *Social adjustment at 11 and legitimacy status*

Independent variables	Dependent variable = Social adjustment at 11 (transformed)			
	F Constant	SE	DF	χ^2
Overall constant	3.20			
Legitimacy status				
Illegitimate	0.09		2	28.7***
Adopted	0.22			
Legitimate	−0.31			
Sex: Male/female	0.48	0.03	1	283.1***
Social class				
Origin *11*				
NM NM	−0.32		5	131.9***
M M	0.12			
NM M	0.08			
M NM	−0.15			
NM NMH	0.12			
M NMH	0.15			
Number of children				
1–2	−0.18		2	56.5***
3–4	−0.04			
5+	0.22			
Free school meals/not	0.42	0.06	1	57.8***
Crowding: ≤ 1.5– > 1.5	−0.08	0.06	1	2.2
Amenities				
Sole use 3	−0.14		3	29.5***
Sole use 2	0.12			
Sole use 1	0.16			
Sole use 0	−0.14			
Interactions				
Legitimacy status by sex			2	3.9
Sex by social class			5	3.4
Legitimacy status by no. of children			4	10.7*
Legitimacy status by crowding			2	0.0
Legitimacy status by social class †			8	3.3
(a) Fitting all main effects				
Illeg–legit	0.40	0.10	2	17.3***
Adop–legit	0.53	0.15	2	12.1**
Illeg–adop	−0.13	0.18	2	0.5
Sample size	9 242			
Total variance	2.06			
Residual mean square	1.89			
Dependent variable mean	2.52			

continued overleaf

TABLE A14.1–continued

Independent variables	Dependent variable = Social adjustment at 11 (transformed)			
	F constant	SE	DF	χ^2
Fitting legitimacy status alone				
Overall constant	2.81	(N)		
Illegitimate	0.23	(198)	2	32.0***
Adopted	0.07	(80)		
Legitimate	−0.30	(8 964)		
(b) Fitting legitimacy status alone				
Illeg–legit	0.53	0.10	2	27.0**
Adop–legit	0.37	0.16	2	5.3
Illeg–adop	0.16	0.19	2	0.7

Fitted constants for interaction – legitimacy status by number of children adjusted for other variables in the analysis

No. of children	Legitimacy status		
	Illeg	Adopted	Legit
1–2	0.01	0.37	−0.22
3–4	0.52	0.59	−0.08
5+	0.60	−1.97	0.19

† There are 8df for this interaction, as there were no adopted children in either of the last two categories of the social class variable.

TABLE A14.2 *Social adjustment at 11 and family situation*

Independent variables	Dependent variable = Social adjustment (transformed)			
	F Constant	SE	DF	χ^2
Overall constant	3.12			
Family situation and legitimacy status				
(a) Legit 2NP 7 and 11	− 0.36		4	27.8***
(b) Legit step 7 and 11	− 0.10			
(c) Adopted 7 and 11	0.14			
(d) Illeg 2NP 7 and 11	0.06			
(e) Illeg step 7 and 11	0.26			
Sex: Boy–Girl	0.47	0.03	1	247.5***
Social class				
Origin *11*				
NM NM	− 0.24		3	109.5***
M M	0.18			
NM M	0.14			
M NM	− 0.08			
Number of children				
1–2	− 0.18		2	48.9***
3–4	− 0.05			
5 +	0.23			
Free school meals/not	0.38	0.06	1	35.1***
Crowding: ⩽ 1.5–> 1.5	− 0.11	0.06	1	3.0
Amenities				
Sole use 3	− 0.09		3	21.5***
Sole use 2	0.16			
Sole use 1	0.13			
Sole use 0	− 0.20			
Interaction				
Family situation and legitimacy status by sex			4	8.5
For family situation and legitimacy status				
(a) vs each of (b)–(e)				
(a)–(b)	− 0.26	0.15	1	2.8
Fitting (a)–(c)	− 0.50	0.16	1	9.8**
all main (a)–(d)	− 0.42	0.16	1	7.3**
effects (a)–(e)	− 0.62	0.21	1	8.7**

continued overleaf

TABLE A14.2–continued

Independent variables	Dependent variable = Social adjustment (transformed)			
	F Constant	SE	DF	χ^2
Sample size	8 228			
Total variance	2.02			
Residual mean square	1.87			
Dependent variable mean	2.48			
Fit family situation and legitimacy status alone				
Overall constant	2.9	(N)		
(a) Legit 2NP 7 and 11	− 0.40	(7 954)	4	31.0***
(b) Legit step 7 and 11	− 0.05	(81)		
(c) Adopted 7 and 11	− 0.01	(74)		
(d) Illeg 2NP 7 and 11	0.12	(77)		
(e) Illeg step 7 and 11	0.34	(42)		
For family situation and legitimacy status				
(a) vs each of (b)–(e)				
Fitting family (a)–(b)	− 0.35	0.16	1	4.9*
situation and (a)–(c)	− 0.38	0.16	1	5.4*
legitimacy (a)–(d)	− 0.52	0.16	1	10.3***
status alone: (a)–(e)	− 0.74	0.22	1	11.2***

TABLE A14.3   *Changes in BSAG 7–11 and legitimacy status*

Independent variables	Dependent variable = Social adjustment at 11 (transformed)			
	F Constant	SE	DF	χ^2
Overall constant	2.03			
7-year score (measured about mean)	0.38	0.01	1	1 462.0***
Legitimacy status				
Illegitimate	−0.03		2	21.6***
Adopted	0.31			
Legitimate	−0.28			
Sex: Boy–Girl	0.31	0.03	1	132.2***
Social class				
Origin 11				
NM NM	−0.28		5	81.0***
M M	0.06			
NM M	0.05			
M NM	−0.11			
NM NMH	0.15			
M NMH	0.13			
Number of children				
1–2	−0.14		2	39.6***
3–4	−0.01			
5+	0.15			
Free school meals/not	0.24	0.05	1	20.8***
Crowding: ⩽ 1.5– > 1.5	−0.04	0.05	1	0.7
Amenities				
Sole use of 3	−0.07		3	22.1***
Sole use of 2	0.11			
Sole use of 1	0.18			
Sole use of 0	−0.22			
Interactions				
Legitimacy status by sex			2	1.4
Legitimacy status by 7-year score			2	1.1
Sample size	8 999			
Total variance	2.06			
Residual mean square	1.62			
Dependent variable mean	2.52			

continued overleaf

TABLE A14.3–continued

Independent variables	Dependent variable = Social adjustment at 11 (transformed)			
	F Constant	SE	DF	χ^2
Fit legitimacy status and 7-year score alone				
7-year score	0.43	0.01	1	1 901.0***
Legitimacy status				
Illegitimate	0.05		2	19.4***
Adopted	0.22			
Legitimate	−0.27			
Interaction				
Legitimacy status by 7-year score			2	0.6
Fit legitimacy status, 7-year score and other variables (as in full model above) with reliability† of 7-year score = 0.9 (0.8)	*Fitted constants*			
Legitimacy status				
Illegitimate	−0.04 (−0.06)			
Adopted	0.31 (0.31)			
Legitimate	−0.27 (−0.25)			

† See Appendix 1 for discussion of reliability of 7-year scores.

Appendix 3
List of Supplementary Tables

Copies are obtainable at cost price from the Supplementary Publications Scheme, British Library (Lending Division), Boston Spa, Yorkshire LS23 7BO, quoting reference number SUP 81007. A set is also available for reference in the library at the National Children's Bureau, 8 Wakley Street, London EC1V 7QE.

S13.2   (i) Reading at 11 (ii) Maths at 11, legitimacy and family size (AOV)
S13.3   (i) Reading at 11 (ii) Maths at 11, legitimacy and free school meals (AOV)
S13.4   (i) Reading at 11 (ii) Maths at 11, legitimacy and crowding (AOV)
S13.5   (i) Reading at 11 (ii) Maths at 11, legitimacy and amenities (AOV)
S13.6   (i) Reading at 11 (ii) Maths at 11, raw scores at 11
S13.7   Reading at 11, mean scores in cells; social class origin/11 and family situation at 7
S13.8   Reading at 11, mean scores in cells; social class origin/11 and family situation at 11
S13.9   Reading at 11, mean scores in cells; social class origin/11 and family size at 11
S13.10 Reading at 11, (a) financial situation (b) crowding (c) amenities
S13.11 Reading at 11, mean scores in cells; social class origin/11 and family situation 7 and 11
S13.12 Reading at 11, mean scores (a) for analysis by legitimacy status (b) for analysis by family situation
S13.13 Maths at 11, mean scores in cells; social class origin/11 and family situation at 7
S13.14 Maths at 11, mean scores in cells; social class origin/11 and family situation at 11
S13.15 Maths at 11, mean scores in cells; social class origin/11 and family size at 11
S13.16 Maths at 11, mean scores in cells; social class origin/11 and (a) financial situation (b) crowding (c) amenities
S13.17 Maths at 11, mean scores in cells; social class origin/11 and family situation at 7 and 11
S13.18 Maths at 11, mean scores (a) for analysis by legitimacy status (b) for analysis by family situation
S14.1   BSAG at 11, legitimacy status, sex and social class (AOV)
S14.2   BSAG at 11, legitimacy status and family size (AOV)
S14.3   BSAG at 11, legitimacy status and free school meals (AOV)
S14.4   BSAG at 11, legitimacy status and crowding (AOV)
S14.5   BSAG at 11, legitimacy status and access to amenities
S14.6   BSAG at 11, mean scores in cells; social class origin/11 and family situation at 7
S14.7   BSAG at 11, mean scores in cells; social class origin/11 and family situation at 11
S14.8   BSAG at 11, mean scores in cells; social class origin/11 and family size at 11
S14.9   BSAG at 11, mean scores in cells; social class origin/11 and (a) financial situation (b) crowding (c) amenities
S14.10 BSAG at 11, mean scores in cells, social class origin/11 and family situation at 7 and 11
S14.11 BSAG at 11, mean scores (a) for analysis by legitimacy status (b) for analysis by family situation

Bibliography

Abel-Smith, B. and Townsend, P. (1965) *The Poor and the Poorest* (London: Bell).

Ainsworth, M. D. (1964) 'Patterns of attachment behaviour shown by the infant in interaction with his mother', *Merill-Palmer Quarterly*, 10, 51–8.

Askham, J. (1975) *Fertility and Deprivation: a study of differential fertility amongst working-class families in Aberdeen* (London: Cambridge University Press).

Banfield, J., Bowyer, C. and Wilkie, E. (1966) 'Parents and education', *Educational Research*, 9, 1, 63–6.

Becker, H. S. (1960) *Outsiders: Studies in the Sociology of Deviance* (New York: Free Press).

Bell, C. (1972) 'Marital status' in P. Barker (ed.), *A Sociological Portrait* (Harmondsworth: Penguin).

Bernstein, B. (1961) 'Social structure, language and learning', *Educational Research*, 3, 163–76.

Bernstein, B. (1966) 'Elaborated and restricted codes: their social origins and some consequences' in A. G. Smith (ed.), *Communication and Culture* (New York: Holt, Rinehart and Winston).

Bhapkar, V. P. (1968) 'On the analysis of contingency tables with a quantitative response', *Biometrics*, 24, 329–38.

Birdwhistell, R. C. (1966) 'The American family: some perspectives', *Psychiatry*, 29, 3, 203–12.

Blake, P. (1972) *The Plight of One-Parent Families* (London: Council for Children's Welfare).

Bohman, M. (1970) *Adopted Children and their Families: a Follow-up Study of Adopted Children, their Background, Environment and Adjustment* (Stockholm: Proprius).

Bohman, M. (1971) 'A comparative study of adopted children, foster children and children in their biological environment born after undesired pregnancies', *Acta Paediatrica Scandanavica*, suppl. 221.

Bottomley, V. (1972) *Families with Low Income in London* (London: CPAG).

Bowlby, J. (1951) *Maternal Care and Mental Health* (Geneva: WHO).

Brenner, R. F. (1951) *A Follow-up Study of Adoptive Families* (New York: Child Adoption Research Committee).

Bronfenbrenner, U. (1958) 'Socialization and social class through time and space' in E. E. Maccoby *et al.* (eds), *Readings in Social Psychology* (New York: Holt, Rinehart and Winston).

Brown, G. W. and Harris, T. (1978) *Social Origins of Depression* (London: Tavistock).

Brown, M. (1974) *Poor Families and Inflation* (London: CPAG).

Bull, D. (ed.) (1971) *Family Poverty* (London: Duckworth/CPAG).

Butler, N. R. and Bonham, D. G. (1963) *Perinatal Mortality* (Edinburgh: Livingstone).

Caldwell, B. M. (1970) 'The effects of psychological deprivation on human development in infancy', *Merill-Palmer Quarterly*, 16, 260–77.

Carlsmith, L. (1964) 'Effect of early father absence on scholastic aptitude', *Harvard Educational Review*, 34, 1–21.

Catholic Housing Aid Society (1972) *Evidence to the Finer Committee on One Parent Families* (London: CHAS).

Central Advisory Council for Education (England) (1967) *Children and Their Primary Schools*, 2 vols (Chairman: Lady Plowden) (London: HMSO).

Central Statistical Office (1978) *Social Trends*, No. 9 (London: HMSO).

Chamberlain, R. *et al.* (1975) *British Births (1970)*, vol. 1 (London: Heinemann Medical).

Chester, R. (1971) 'Contemporary trends in the stability of English marriage', *Journal of Biosocial Science*, 3, 389–402.

Chester, R. (1976(a)) 'Youth, marriage and divorce', *Youth in Society*, 18 4–6.

Chester, R. (1976(b)) 'Divorce laws and the one-parent family', *Concern*, 20, 24–8.

Child Adoption (1975) 'The background to the quest for an adoptive child: the struggle for fertility', *Child Adoption*, 82, 35–40.

Clarke, A. M. and Clarke, A. D. B. (eds) (1974) *Mental Deficiency: the Changing Outlook*, 3rd ed. (London: Methuen).

Clarke, A. M. and Clarke, A. D. B. (1976) *Early Experience* (London: Open Books).

Cogswell, B. E. (1975) 'Variant family forms and life styles: rejection of the traditional nuclear family', *Family Co-ordinator*, 24, 4, 391–406.

Cooper, J. D. (1974) 'Dimensions of parenthood' in Department of Health and Social Security, *The Family in Society* (London: HMSO).

Crellin, E., Pringle, M. L. K. and West, P. (1971) *Born Illegitimate* (Windsor: NFER).

Davie, R., Butler, N. R. and Goldstein, H. (1972) *From Birth to Seven* (London: Longman in assoc. with NCB).

Davis, K. (1939) 'Illegitimacy and the social structure', *American Journal of Sociology*, 45, 215–33.

Davis, K. (1948) *Human Society* (New York: Macmillan).

Department of Employment and Productivity (1970) *Family Expenditure Survey, Report for 1969* (London: HMSO).

Department of the Environment (1971) *Report of the Committee on the Rent*

Acts (Chairman: H. E. Francis) (London: HMSO).
Department of Health and Social Security (1974) *Report of the Committee on One-Parent Families*, 2 vols (Chairman: Hon. Sir Morris Finer) (London: HMSO).
Donnison, D. V. (1967) *The Government of Housing* (Harmondsworth: Penguin Books).
Douglas, J. W. B. (1964) *The Home and the School* (London: MacGibbon and Kee).
Douglas, J. W. B. and Simpson, H. (1964) 'Height in relation to puberty, family size and social class', *Milbank Memorial Fund Quarterly*, 42, 3, 20–35.
Douglas, J. W. B., Ross, J. M. and Simpson, H. R. (1968) *All our Future* (London: Peter Davies).
Edmonds, J. and Radice, G. (1968) *Low Pay* (London: Fabian Society).
Essen, J. and Parrinder, D. (1975) 'Housing for children: further findings from the NCDS', *Housing Review*, 24, 4, 112–14.
Essen, J. and Ghodsian, M. (1977) 'Sixteen-year-olds in households in receipt of Supplementary Benefit and Family Income Supplement' in Supplementary Benefits Commission, *Annual Report* (London: HMSO).
Essen, J. and Lambert, L. (1977) 'Living in one-parent families: relationships and attitudes of 16-year-olds', *Child: Care, health and development*, 3, 5, 301–18.
Essen, J. and Fogelman, K. (1979) 'Childhood housing experiences', *Concern*, 32, 5–10.
Ferri, E. (1976) *Growing-up in a One Parent Family* (Windsor: NFER).
Ferri, E. and Robinson, H. (1976) *Coping Alone* (Windsor: NFER).
Field, F. (1974) *Unequal Britain: a Report on the Cycle of Inequality* (London: Arrow Books).
Fletcher, R. (1962) *The Family and Marriage* (Harmondsworth: Penguin).
Floud, J. E., Halsey, A. H. and Martin, F. M. (1956) *Social Class and Educational Opportunity* (London: Heinemann).
Fogarty, M. P., Rapoport, R. and Rapoport, R. N. (1971) *Sex, Career and Family* (London: Allen and Unwin).
Fogelman, K. R. (1975) 'Developmental correlates of family size', *British Journal of Social Work*, 5, 1, 43–57.
Fogelman, K. (ed.) (1976) *Britain's Sixteen Year Olds* (London: National Children's Bureau).
Fogelman, K. R. and Goldstein, H. (1976) 'Social factors associated with changes in educational attainment between 7 and 11 years of age', *Educational Studies*, 2, 2, 95–109.
Fogelman, K. *et al.* (1978) 'Patterns of attainment', *Educational Studies*, 4, 2, 121–30.
Gabriel, K. R. (1966) 'Simultaneous test procedures for multiple comparisons on categorical data', *Journal of the American Statistical Association*, 61, 1081–96.
Galbraith, J. K. (1958) *Affluent Society* (London: Hamish Hamilton).
George, V. (1974) 'Social security and one parent families', *Poverty*, 28, 2–5.
George, V. and Wilding, P. (1972) *Motherless Families* (London: Routledge and Kegan Paul).

Gill, D. G. (1977) *Illegitimacy, Sexuality and the Status of Women* (Oxford: Blackwell).

Glastonbury, B. (1971) *Homeless Near a Thousand Homes. A Study of Families Without Homes in South Wales and the West of England* (London: Allen and Unwin).

Goldfarb, W. (1943) 'The effects of early institutional care on adolescent personality', *Journal of Experimental Education*, 12, 106–29.

Goode, W. J. (1964) *The Family* (Englewood Cliffs, N.J.: Prentice-Hall).

Grant, M. W. (1964) 'Rate of growth in relation to birth rank and family size', *British Journal of Preventive and Social Medicine*, 18, 35–42.

Greve, J. (1964) *London's Homeless* (London: Bell).

Greve, J., Page, D. and Greve, S. (1971) *Homelessness in London* (Edinburgh: Scottish Academic Press).

Grey, E. and Blunden, R. M. (1971) *A Survey of Adoption in Great Britain* (London: HMSO).

Harris, C. (1969) *The Family* (London: Allen and Unwin).

Hartley, S. F. (1975) *Illegitimacy* (Berkeley: University of California Press).

Helfer, R. E. and Kempe, C. H. (eds) (1968) *The Battered Child* (University of Chicago Press).

Herzog, E. and Sudia, C. E. (1968) 'Fatherless homes: a review of research', *Children*, 15, 5, 177–82.

Holman, R. (ed.) (1970a) *Socially Deprived Families in Britain* (London: Bedford Square Press of NCSS).

Holman, R. (1970b) *Unsupported Mothers and the Care of their Children* (London: Mothers in Action).

Holman, R. (1973) 'Poverty: consensus and alternatives', *British Journal of Social Work*, 3, 4, 431–46.

Holman, R. (1975) 'Unmarried mothers, social deprivation and child separation', *Policy and Politics*, 3, 4, 25–41.

Holman, R. (1976) *Inequality in Child Care*, Poverty Pamphlet No. 26 (London: CPAG).

Humphrey, M. (1969) *The Hostage Seekers – a Study of Childless and Adopting Couples* (London: Longman/NCB).

Hunt, A., Fox, J. and Morgan, M. (1973) *Families and Their Needs*, 2 vols (London: HMSO).

Illsley, R. (1955) 'Social class selection and class differences in relation to still births and infant deaths', *British Medical Journal*, ii, 1520–24.

Jacka, A. (1973) *Adoption in Brief* (Windsor: NFER).

Jackson, B. and Jones, J. (1971) *One Thousand Children* (Cambridge: ACE).

Jaffee, B. and Fanshel, D. (1970) *How They Fared in Adoption: a Follow-up Study* (New York: Columbia University Press).

Jordan, B. (1974) *Poor Parents, Social Policy and the 'Cycle of Deprivation'* (London: Routledge and Kegan Paul).

Kadushin, A. (1970) *Adopting Older Children* (New York: Columbia University Press).

Kirk, H. D. (1964) *Shared Fate* (New York: Free Press).

Kohn, M. L. (1963) 'Social class and parent-child relationships: an interpretation', *American Journal of Sociology*, 68, 4, 471–80.

Kornitzer, M. (1968) *Adoption and Family Life* (London: Putnam).

Kriesberg, L. (1963) 'The relationship between socio-economic rank and behaviour', *Social Problems*, 10, 4, 334–53.

Kriesberg, L. (1970) *Mothers in Poverty* (Chicago: Aldine).

Labov, W. (1969) 'The logic of non-standard English', *Georgetown Monograph on Language and Linguistics*, 22, 1.31.

Lambert, R. (1964) *Nutrition in Britain, 1950–1960* (Welwyn: Codicote Press).

Land, H. (1969) *Large Families in London* (London: Bell).

Laslett, P. (1972) *Household and Family in Past Time* (London: Cambridge University Press).

Lawder, E. A. (1970) 'Postadoption counseling: a professional obligation', *Child Welfare*, 49, 8, 435–42.

Leahy, A. (1933) 'Some characteristics of adoptive parents', *American Journal of Sociology*, 38, 548–63.

Lewin, K. (1948) 'Bringing up the Jewish Child' in K. Lewin, *Resolving Social Conflicts* (New York: Harper and Row).

Lewis, H. (1954) *Deprived Children, the Mersham Experiment; a Social and Clinical Study* (London: Oxford University Press for Nuffield Foundation).

Lewis, O. (1959) *Five Families* (New York: Basic Books).

Lister, R. (1974) *Take-Up of Means Tested Benefits*, Poverty Pamphlet No. 18 (London: CPAG).

Lynes, T. (1969) 'The dinner money problem', *The Guardian*, reprinted in *Poverty*, 10, 13–15.

McWhinnie, A. M. (1967) *Adopted Children: How They Grow Up* (London: Routledge and Kegan Paul).

Maddox, B. (1975) *The Half Parent: Living with Other People's Children* (London: Deutsch).

Malinowski, B. (1964) 'The principle of legitimacy: parenthood, the basis of the social structure' in R. L. Coser, (ed.) *The Family: Its Structures and Functions* (New York: St. Martin's Press).

Mandell, B. R. (1973) *Where are the children? A class analysis of foster care and adoption* (Lexington, Mass.: D. C. Heath).

Mapstone, E. (1969) 'Children in care', *Concern*, 3, 23–8.

Marsden, D. (1973) *Mothers Alone: Poverty and the Fatherless Family*, rev. ed. (Harmondsworth: Penguin).

Middleton, N. (1971) *When Family Failed* (London: Gollancz).

Miller, F. J. W. *et al.* (1974) *The School Years in Newcastle-upon-Tyne 1952–62* (London: Oxford University Press).

Ministry of Housing and Local Goverment (1965) *Report of the Committee on Housing in Greater London* (Chairman: Sir Milner Holland) (London: HMSO).

Ministry of Housing and Local Government (1969) *Council Housing, Purposes, Procedures and Priorities* (Chairman: J. B. Cullingworth) (London: HMSO).

Ministry of Social Security (1967) *Circumstances of Families: Report on an Enquiry by the Ministry of Pensions and National Insurance with the Co-operation of the NAB* (London: HMSO).

Moore, B. (1969) 'Thoughts on the future of the family' in J. N. Edwards (ed.), *The Family and Change* (New York: Knopf).

Nash, R. (1973) *Classrooms Observed: the Teacher's Perception and the*

188   *Bibliography*

Pupil's Performance (London: Routledge and Kegan Paul).

Nemovicher, J. (1959) *A Comparative Study of Adopted Boys and Non-Adopted in Respect of Specific Personality Characteristics*, D. Phil. Thesis (School of Education, New York University).

Newson, E. and Newson, J. (1963) *Infant Care in an Urban Community* (London: Allen and Unwin).

Newson, J. and Newson, E. (1974) 'Cultural aspects of child-rearing in the English-speaking world' in M. P. M. Richards (ed.), *The Integration of a Child into a Social World* (London: Cambridge University Press).

Newson, J. and Newson, E. (1976) *Seven Years Old in the Home Environment* (London: Allen and Unwin).

Nisbet, J. and Entwistle, N. J. (1967) 'Intelligence and family size, 1949–1965', *British Journal of Educational Psychology*, 37, 2, 188–93.

Office of Population Censuses and Surveys (1973) *The General Household Survey: Introductory Report . . .* (London: HMSO).

Oliver, J. E. *et al.* (1974) *Severely Ill-Treated Young Children in North-East Wiltshire*, Research Report No. 4 (Oxford University Unit of Clinical Epidemiology).

Orshansky, M. (1963) 'Children of the poor', *Social Security Bulletin*, 26, 7, 3–12.

Packman, J. (1968) *Child Care: Needs and Numbers* (London: Allen and Unwin).

Parsons, T. (1949) 'The social structure of the family' in R. N. Anshen (ed.), *The Family: Its Function and Destiny* (New York: Harper and Row).

Parsons, T. and Bales, R. F. (1956) *Family, Socialization and Interaction Process* (London: Routledge and Kegan Paul).

Pilling, D. and Pringle, M. L. K. (1978) *Controversial Issues in Child Development* (London: Elek).

Pinchbeck, I. (1954) 'Social attitudes to the problem of illegitimacy', *British Journal of Sociology*, 5, 309–24.

Pinker, R. A. (1971) *Social Theory and Social Policy* (London: Heinemann).

Pochin, J. (1969) *Without a Wedding Ring* (London: Constable).

Pohlman, E. (1970) 'Childlessness, intentional and unintentional: psychological and social aspects', *Journal of Nervous and Mental Disease*, 151, 1, 2–12.

Pringle, M. L. K. (1967) *Adoption – Facts and Fallacies* (London: Longman/NCB).

Pringle, M. L. K. (1971) *Deprivation and Education*, 2nd ed. (London: Longman/NCB).

Pringle, M. L. K. (1974) *The Needs of Children* (London: Hutchinson).

Pritchard, C. and Butler, A. (1975) 'Influence of the youth tutor upon teachers' perception of some maladjusted behaviour', *Child Care: Health and Development*, 1, 4, 251–61.

Rainwater, L. (1965) *Family Design, Marital Sexuality, Family Size and Family Planning* (Chicago: Aldine).

Rapoport, R. *et al.* (1977) *Fathers, Mothers and Others* (London: Routledge and Kegan Paul).

Raynor, L. (1980) *The Adopted Child Comes of Age* (London, Allen and Unwin).

Roberts, R. W. (ed.) (1966) *The Unwed Mother* (New York: Harper and Row).

Rodman, H. (1963) 'The lower class value stretch', *Social Forces*, 42, 2, 205–15.

Rowe, J. (1970) 'The realities of adoptive parenthood', *Child Adoption*, 59, 23–9.

Rowe, J. and Lambert, L. (1973) *Children Who Wait* (London: Association of British Adoption Agencies).

Rowntree, B. S. (1901) *Poverty: a Study of Town Life* (London: Macmillan).

Rutter, M. L., Tizard, J. and Whitmore, K. (eds) (1970) *Education, Health and Behaviour* (London: Longman).

Rutter, M. (1972) *Maternal Deprivation Reassessed* (Harmondsworth: Penguin).

Rutter, M. (1974) 'A critical note. Review of "Born Illegitimate" and "Growing-up Adopted"', *Journal of Child Psychology and Psychiatry*, 15, 2, 149–51.

Rutter, M. and Madge, N. (1976) *Cycles of Disadvantage* (London: Heinemann).

Ryan, W. (1971) *Blaming the Victim* (New York: Pantheon).

Sants, H. J. (1964) 'Genealogical bewilderment in children with substitute parents', *British Journal of Medical Psychology*, 37, 2, 133–41.

Scheffé, M. A. (1959) *The Analysis of Variables* (New York: Wiley).

Schlesinger, B. (1966) 'The one parent family: an overview', *Family Life Co-ordinator*, 15, 133–8.

Schlesinger, B. (1969) *The One Parent Family: Perspectives and Annotated Bibliography* (University of Toronto Press).

Schorr, A. L. (1964) *Slums and Social Insecurity* (London: Nelson).

Seglow, J., Pringle, M. L. K. and Wedge, P. J. (1972) *Growing-up Adopted* (Windsor: NFER).

Sinfield, A. (1968) *The Long-Term Unemployed* (Paris: OECD).

Skeels, H. M. and Harms, I. (1948) 'Children with inferior social histories: their mental development in adoptive homes', *Journal of Genetic Psychology*, 72, 283–94.

Skolnick, A. S. (1973) *The Intimate Environment: Exploring Marriage and the Family* (Boston, Mass.: Little, Brown).

Skolnick, A. and Skolnick J. W. (1974) *Intimacy, Family and Society* (Boston, Mass.: Little, Brown).

Southgate, V. (1962) *Southgate Group Reading Tests: Manual of Instructions* (University of London Press).

Spence, J. C. *et al.* (1954) *A Thousand Families in Newcastle-upon-Tyne* (London: Oxford University Press).

Spencer, K. (1970) 'Housing and socially deprived families' in R. Holman (ed.), *Socially Deprived Families in Britain* (London: Bedford Square Press of NCSS).

Spitz, R. A. (1946) 'Hospitalism: a follow-up report', *Psychoanalytic Study of the Child*, 2, 313–42.

Sprey, J. (1969) 'The study of single parenthood: some methodological considerations' in Schlesinger, B., *The One Parent Family: Perspectives and Annotated Bibliography* (Toronto University Press).

Stott, D. H. (1966) *The Social Adjustment of Children. Manual to the Bristol Social Adjustment Guides*, 3rd ed. (University of London Press).

Supplementary Benefits Commission (1967) *The Administration of the Wage Stop: Report of the Supplementary Benefits Commission to the Minister of Social Security* (Chairman: R. Hayward) (London: HMSO).

Tanner, J. M., Goldstein, H. and Whitehouse, R. H. (1970) 'Standards for children's height at ages 2–9 years, allowing for height of parents', *Archives of Diseases in Childhood*, 45, 755–62.

Titmuss, R. M. (1958) *Essays on the Welfare State* (London: Allen and Unwin).

Tizard, B. (1977) *Adoption: a Second Chance* (London: Open Books).

Townsend, P. (ed.) (1970) *The Concept of Poverty* (London: Heinemann).

Triseliotis, J. (1973) *In Search of Origins* (London: Routledge and Kegan Paul).

Tunnard, J. (1977) 'Housing advice notes', *Roof*, 2, 2, 61–4.

Turner, C. (1969) *Family and Kinship in Modern Britain* (London: Routledge and Kegan Paul).

Valentine, C. A. (1968) *Culture of Poverty: Critique and Counter-Proposals* (University of Chicago Press).

Vincent, C. E. (1961) *Unmarried Mothers* (New York: Free Press of Glencoe).

Waller, W. W. (1951) *The Family: a dynamic interpretation*, rev. ed. (New York: Dryden Press).

Warren, R. D., White, J. K. and Fuller, W. A. (1974) 'An errors-in-variables analysis of managerial role performance', *Journal of the American Statistical Association*, 69, 886.

Wedderburn, D. and Craig, C. (1974) 'Relative deprivation in work', in Wedderburn, D. (ed.), *Poverty, Inequality and Class Structure* (London: Cambridge University Press).

Wedge, P. (1969) 'The second follow-up of the National Child Development Study', *Concern*, 3, 34–9.

Wedge, P. and Prosser, H. (1973) *Born to Fail?* (London: Arrow/NCB).

Weinstein, E. A. and Geisel, P. M. (1960) 'An analysis of sex differences in adjustment', *Child Development*, 31, 721–8.

West, D. J. and Farrington, D. P. (1973) *Who Becomes Delinquent?* (London: Heinemann).

Willmott, P. and Young, M. (1960) *Family and Class in a London Suburb* (London: Routledge and Kegan Paul).

Wilson, H. (1970) 'The socialization of children' in Holman, R. (ed.), *Socially Deprived Families in Britain* (London, Bedford Square Press of NCSS).

Wilson, H. and Herbert, G. W. (1978) *Parents and Children in the Inner City* (London: Routledge and Kegan Paul).

Wimperis, V. (1960) *The Unmarried Mother and her Child* (London: Allen and Unwin).

Woolf, M. (1967) *The Housing Survey in England and Wales, 1964* (London: HMSO).

Wynn, M. (1964) *Fatherless Families* (London: Michael Joseph).

Young, L. (1954) *Out of Wedlock* (New York: McGraw-Hill).

Young, M. and Willmott, P. (1973) *The Symmetrical Family* (London: Routledge and Kegan Paul).

Yudkin, S. and Holme, A. (1963) *Working Mothers and their Children* (London: Michael Joseph).

Index

Page numbers in *italics* refer to a table or figure. Where a reference is continuous over several pages, tables have not been numbered separately (see pp. ix–x for lists).